SEEING THINGS...
PREDICTING RESULTS

The Professional Lives
of Five Working Psychics

PAT HANNA

 FriesenPress

Suite 300 - 990 Fort St
Victoria, BC, Canada, V8V 3K2
www.friesenpress.com

Copyright © 2015 by Pat Hanna
First Edition — 2015

All rights reserved.

No part of this publication may be reproduced in any form, or by any means, electronic or mechanical, including photocopying, recording, or any information browsing, storage, or retrieval system, without permission in writing from FriesenPress.

ISBN
978-1-4602-7492-7 (Paperback)
978-1-4602-7493-4 (eBook)

1. Biography & Autobiography

Distributed to the trade by The Ingram Book Company

DEDICATION

For my husband, Wally
whose patience, tolerance, help and love made this work possible. And to our Deb, Keith, Dean and David, who continue to inspire and to Michael, who never fails to listen and encourage.

PREFACE

The idea presented itself as the challenge of a writer's lifetime of work . . . find and interview five psychics, then delve into their minds and try to determine what makes a psychic tick. The problem at the beginning was my own disbelief and reservation that any such people existed and if they did so claim they were paranormal, what could they do or say that would make me a believer.

It was then I decided if I should connect with these psychics, I would at the conclusion of each interview ask each of them the same question, but only one which would relate to an event that was to occur in my life. However; I would not ask until the last word was written.

This I did! Each psychic was asked the same question and each one readily replied. You, however, Dear Reader, will have to wait to the end of this book to learn exactly what that question is, and how each psychic replied.

You can fast forward, of course, nothing to stop you from doing this, but alternatively, you might prefer the challenge to read the book through and then decide if you believe in the paranormal. You can determine what in this narrative is to you, genuine and true.

I hope you will enjoy the journey.

THE BEGINNING

On that lovely spring day, the luncheon began as they always do with warm greetings and gentle hugs from one lady to the next and chatter at a maximum, but momentarily everyone at the table suddenly fell silent as each one contemplated the next topic of conversation. Soon one of the participants asked, "Has any of you ever been to a psychic?" An extraordinary hush descended, and a finely tuned ear would hear if listening that each lady seemed hesitant and held back any comment, perhaps in fear of ridicule but also obviously waiting for another to be the first to reply.

No one spoke, so I said, "No, I have not, and furthermore, I am completely skeptical and doubt that anyone who will claim to be a so-called paranormal practitioner, could well be both a charlatan and dishonest. Consider if you will, several of whom have been showcased on television and you can readily discern their obvious and pseudo personas."

2-

Suddenly conversational mayhem prevailed as everyone began to speak at once, with several admitting they had been to one and completely supported the gift that psychics exhibited, but there were others who agreed with me and felt these 'so-called paranormal intellectuals' were dishonest, would often target the downtrodden in society and demand atrocious and exorbitant fees for their services.

One factor was clearly evident.

This marked the first time one of our luncheons lasted four hours and it was also the first time one of our conversations became as animated and intense as it did on this day. As we said goodbye, it was apparent we had reached a consensus that each one wanted to continue this conversation as quickly as possible, so plans were tentatively set for a future meeting. We would, with alacrity, continue to explore the mystical world of psychic phenomena.

The rest of that day and into the evening, our boisterous conversation stayed with me and got me to thinking about the paranormal world about which I knew nothing. I had neither met nor spoken to a psychic and I had no idea what peculiarities would be associated with this spectral world.

3-

The nearest I had ever come to the paranormal were the ghost stories I had concocted for my grandsons, one called, 'The Ghosts of the Riverhurst Ferry,' ergo; my knowledge and interest in ghosts were almost nonexistent.

My mind that night, even during sleep, would not relinquish its hold, as I mentally explored the mysteries of this subject, so it was by morning my decision was made. I would investigate. I would locate a psychic or several to learn more, in an attempt to dissect this esoteric, mystical, extrasensory sphere.

The result of my research and literary effort is revealed in this narrative, and although I recognize there will be those who will deem this story 'hogwash' which is not my word but rather is the opinion of a well-known radio personality in Calgary, Alberta, who, in talking about psychics, ghosts and the paranormal, emphatically stated they were, each one 'phoney.' Hopefully, there will be others who will be intrigued and are encouraged to read on to discover for themselves what enigmas exist in the world of the 'unnatural.'

PSYCHIC

DON MCGRATH
ST. JOHN'S
NEWFOUNDLAND
CANADA

AUTHOR'S NOTES . . .

In garnering information over numerous sessions with psychic Don McGrath, he gives the impression he is a simple man, an uncomplicated paranormal if there is such a person, but a man who believes his life, his 'gift' and his talent, originates from one source, and one source only. Here is a psychic who claims he lives an uncomplicated life day to day, but the question is, "does he?"

The writer opines his revelation may be slightly erroneous, for I discovered during each of our sessions, there is also a different, more complicated Don, the one who will expend immense energy in his paranormal practice, for each and every client. There are dimensions to him that belie his efforts to live simply, as he strives to use his paranormal powers, in a forthright, honest manner. Don believes God is the source of his 'gift' and the Deity, he believes also has dominion over everything this psychic does. His convictions aren't as fundamental or unproblematic as they may appear, which may become more apparent as you get to know him. His convictions to never abuse God or his clients are commendable, but these sentiments inevitably take their toll for Don does pay a price for his 'gift' as will be revealed in his story. One factor is for certain. He is exceedingly grateful for his 'gift' and comfortable in his liaison with clients, as he diligently and daily strives to live his life ethically and exert his paranormal powers, as God would have him do.

MEET PSYCHIC DON MCGRATH NEWFOUNDLAND

Don McGrath calls St. John's, Newfoundland home, but his psychic world extends far beyond the boundaries of this island, because he has clients scattered far and wide across Canada and beyond. He came to my attention when I happened to mention to a colleague I was about to embark on a project which involved the paranormal.

Lisa's reaction portrayed excitement and enthusiasm as she exclaimed, "I just had a reading with a psychic from Newfoundland and he was incredible and completely accurate, as he related events about me and my life. He mentioned facts he couldn't possibly have known," she enthusiastically claimed, so I asked if she would share additional details. It was then she related how the session had come about, and admitted the reading had actually involved her and three other friends. This, they believed, provided protection from an unknown process which was somewhat frightening that first time around.

My reaction as to how such an experience which would seem to be considerably private and exceedingly personal could be shared with others, so I asked Lisa how it could be that she and her friends would willingly share this intimate event with others. I was immediately challenged, as Lisa explained they had collectively decided they would engage a psychic to have some fun, more as a lark than anything else.

A mutual friend, domiciled in St. John's, intervened and contacted Don McGrath to arrange the collective reading. I was astonished to learn this psychic or any other would be willing to 'read' for four clients in one sitting. I couldn't have been more wrong. Don had no difficulty whatever in consenting to their request and ultimately proceeded to 'read' one immediately after the other.

"But, Lisa," I asked, "how did your friends react to his revelations? Did they feel he was accurate or that he offered pertinent and factual details concerning their lives?"

"Oh yes, they did," she replied, and agreed to ask her friends if they would be willing to speak with me, so I could ascertain their impressions of this event.

"No problem," Lisa replied. They confirmed Lisa's comments were factual. Additional commentary regarding psychic veracity will be revealed in testimonials, and refer to the readings of Don and to other psychics whose stories appear in this book. Lisa divulged certain details about her reading which she claims were precise and embraced her unspoken concerns about problems long present in her life. Problems, she claims, which existed long before her session with Don. When her reading concluded, Lisa experienced a sense of peace, relief and claims those issues which troubled her for so long, have diminished. She remains a client of psychic Don.

The psychic advised her as to when certain problems would resolve with an additional warning that some would take time, but yes, in case you question, he also revealed the exact date and year that such resolutions would occur and accomplished all this by long distance on Skype, with Don miles away. It appears he 'read' Lisa and each one of her friends and to this day, each one of these ladies fully supports his accuracy and his sincerity.

"Who can believe this?" I thought at the time, but it is certain now that I am compelled to contact this man to learn for myself more about him, and what precisely he does in a reading. The how was problematic because his telephone number had been misplaced, the friend of a friend who knew him could not be found, and the internet yielded nothing about him. Finally, I had an email address, and although it required tenacity and determination, followed by numerous email messages, my decision to contact him one more time proved to be favourable. Fate intervened and Don's colleague and partner responded, for it seems he handles the business end of psychic life. Tenacity does procure reward, as finally Don and I connected and began what can now be called an interesting, long-distance relationship and one which over time has evolved into one of trust and respect. Don has accepted my efforts will be to tell his story honestly without changing the meaning of what he has to say. My only request was to implore that he would express his beliefs and proffer honest explanations, regarding the 'gift' used in his daily work.

One can doubt his ability in the paranormal, but I have learned it would be difficult, perhaps even impossible, to question his own belief respecting his 'gift' or the fact that Don does 'read' others in a manner which is not only accurate but uncanny.

You, Reader, will decide for yourself about his ability and 'gift' but no matter what your thoughts might be, you will never alter, diminish, or destroy Don's belief in his 'gift.' His clients substantiate his claims and seem to speak with one voice to extol the extraordinary accomplishments he performed for each one of them. His clients are tremendously loyal, and they are believers, as evidenced by their continuous demand for more and more of Don's 'gift' in their private readings.

THE EVOLUTION OF PSYCHIC

DON MCGRATH
ST. JOHN'S, NFLD.

QUESTION 1

Are you a psychic medium?
   "Yes, I am both."

QUESTION 2

Is there a difference between a psychic and a psychic medium; please define each one?
   "Yes! Yes! There is. They are extremely different," exclaims Don, and "I am 'gifted' with both powers." He explains that as a psychic, "I can actually feel the emotions and feelings of another whether the emotion is anger, joy, worry, or dread, and further, these feelings and vibrations are readily and easily detected by any true psychic. No exceptions," he affirms.
   A medium is also a clairvoyant, Don continues, who has second sight, clear hearing, and perfect understanding of those who dwell on the 'other side.'
   "A medium," he believes "can pick up spirits, even demons, who occupy a different level than we do, and further, a medium also has the ability to connect with those who have passed on. One sees pictures in his mind," Don declares, and it is evident these visions are as real to him, as are photograph albums to the rest of us.

A medium can convey messages to the living and can cleanse or assuage anger or hurt. "For example, if one has lost a loved one or a friend without having resolved bitter issues, I can help them communicate their regret. However," Don warns, "a medium must be extremely careful and cautious because he is equally capable of connecting with demons, whose only intentions are nefarious and malignant."

QUESTION 3A

At what age did you discover you had these wonderful but supernatural 'gifts?'

"Picture this if you can," he responds. "You are five years old; seemingly you are a normal, happy little boy on his way back to the home where I lived in Toronto, after enjoying some fun activities with friends. There is nothing unusual about this, but as I approached my parents' house and began to walk up the stairway to the door, a terrifying creature jumped out from a nearby bush, and nearly frightened me to death."

He vividly recalls this entity wore a mask which he later learned was analogous to an African voodoo mask, and "Unlike me," Don remembers, "this creature wasn't the least bit intimidated." It was then he recognized for the first time that he was different and stresses that "this beast was real, not of this world, and yet, my fear quickly subsided because I felt protected, although I wasn't sure why."

Seeing the beast confirmed he was different, but Don also learned his deviation was a topic not to be discussed with his family. "I can clearly recall at age seven when I had a painful toothache, and my grandfather held a Bible over my head, and told me the pain would end immediately and it did. "It's a miracle I thought at the time, but when I asked for an explanation, my grandmother in stern tones, admonished, 'We do not talk about things like this.' The conversation ended, no explanation was given, but henceforth, I knew instinctively this was a subject to be left unspoken, even within my own family."

Don concludes he ultimately learned the goal of the beast that frightened him and shares the revelation. "The only reason it is on this earth is to draw people to the dark side of life. This world harbours people from every domain, and entities like the beast, are ever present to enlist anyone it can, to the malevolent side.

"There is a war," Don opines, "an endless battle between those who are good and others who are evil, and spirits representing both, are here to recruit others to their side. They often have foreknowledge as to who is susceptible, and it seems ever apparent to me that someone will often be one with psychic ability. Every malevolent entity will covet that individual, and will do anything to recruit people to his side and do it before the angels can stake their claim."

QUESTION 3B

Did your mother or father know you were 'gifted' and if so, did they ever advise then to keep this 'gift' to yourself?

"Never." Indeed Don remembers his parents used to tell stories about ghosts and spirits when he was young, but he never felt frightened or disturbed by these tales. Indeed, he remembers, "They were great fun and enjoyable and to this day, I am much more afraid of people than I am of ghosts and ghosts are a very real part of my daily world and that of my parents."

Don discloses, "I grew up in a family who believed in ghosts and I was to learn my grandfather had the 'gift.' He was a psychic medium and my father was a healer." It is here Don explains in the world of psychic phenomena, he has been told a healer is the seventh son of the seventh son, each one with healing powers. A healer can quickly relate to a client and ascertain the source of present problems in his life, but Don warns, "If one does confer with a healer, when the reading is finished; it is advisable that one does not express gratitude or speak at all. Say nothing and leave immediately." The difference between a spirit and a ghost is discernable, according to Don. "A spirit is a soul at peace, whereas a ghost is someone who has passed over but is not at rest. It is a person, who although dead, has not yet navigated the lighted tunnel we all must go through. This apparition must resolve whatever issues prevailed at the time of death, whether it is anger, an unsolved problem, or even the way in which one passed, because until he does he is trapped between life and death."

Don claims people, who were murdered on Earth, are allowed to immediately cross over, unless at the time of death, the deceased is encumbered with negative issues. "If this is so, then one will remain in limbo until those issues are resolved. Spirits," he warns, "can be dangerous," but adds, "conversely, if one is peaceful and happy at the time of death, his spirit will continue to be, when he ascends to our heavenly home."

QUESTION 4A

Apart from knowing you had the 'gift' what were you like as a child?

    A more pensive Don replies to this question as memories of his childhood surface. "The 'gift' certainly affected my early years," he remembers. "I didn't have a ton of friends or playmates but I did have my younger sister and the support of my Mom. I enjoyed their company and still do, but being alone and occupying myself has never been difficult for me. I am never lonely and even as a child, I seemed to possess an inner peace, which even to this day is still a part of who I am."

QUESTION 4B

Was your childhood ever affected positively or negatively by 'the gift?'

    "Yes, negatively," Don remembers, "when we moved into the house in Toronto, there was no forewarning or knowledge it was a haunted house that would become home to our family. Numerous, inexplicable, unexplained happenings occurred regularly. Cupboard doors opened and closed without assistance, the television turned itself on and off at regular intervals throughout the day and night, and frightening noises and sounds would routinely emanate from the walls. My mother, Mary and my sister, Wendy shared my fear. We frankly did not understand what was happening or why."

    Don recalls he was petrified when these phenomena occurred. "I was thirteen," he recalls, "with no knowledge such paranormal events could manifest, until that is, after our family became acquainted with the lady who lived next door. She was a teacup reader who advised this house was acknowledged to be haunted by an entity and in time we knew this was true. It was there, and it let us know it was. "This spirit seemed to emanate from an old pole lamp in the house. You know the kind so popular during the 1950-60s," Don remembers. "When the lamp was turned to bright, this entity would emerge, seemingly not to do harm, but because the glowing bright light seemed to indicate to him, he was in heaven. We did everything we could," he recalls, "to alter the appearance of the lamp and make him leave. We changed the bulbs, replaced the shade, moved the lamp from place to place, and yet, the spirit continued to emerge whenever it wanted to, and did not hesitate to let us know he was there, as he would constantly turn the lamp on and off."

Finally, Don recalls, the same 'teacup' neighbour advised us to earnestly and regularly pray for the spirit to depart. She said we must continue to order it to leave, and although it took two years, it finally did leave, as evidenced by the silence and peace which remained, along with a lamp that was once again functional.

"This was a chilling experience," he remembers, "and it is true during those two years, I became exceedingly angry with this spirit and with that increasing anger, I also gained strength and courage to deal with him and forcefully admonish him to leave. I told him the control was mine and he was to go." To this day, Don unequivocally believes his unmistakable and aggressive coercion finally dislodged the spirit, after which "our home felt empty but gloriously peaceful."

QUESTION 4C

Did the other children recognize you were different?
"Oh yes, they did," recalls Don. "I was often teased and ridiculed, and frequently told to leave an area and play somewhere else. But the mocking and badgering only made me stronger, more confident of who I was and what I could accomplish in my life. This might sound implausible," he admits, "but it is true. My inner strength seemed to intensify and become more prominent following each incident. Other kids around me at the time did not understand me, and as a consequence, they were mean-spirited and harsh."

QUESTION 4D

What were your teen years like?
"I was a loner," Don replies, "but I was never lonely. I never doubted myself, and frequently when others were out having fun, I stayed home to read or watch horror movies. I know this sounds singular and perhaps even antisocial, but for

me it was normal, it was my choice, and it was the way I wanted to live my life, even back then in those early years."

Don's teen years were much similar to his younger years, but as he relates incidents from his childhood, his recollections exemplify firmness and resolve that developed during childhood and have only grown stronger with the passing years. He is his own person, and nothing on this earth will alter this fact, as far as Don is concerned.

QUESTION 5

How did the revelation that you possessed this 'gift' make itself evident to you?

"I didn't realize that other kids didn't have this 'gift' when I was young," Don says, "but I recall how I came to know I did, and as esoteric as it might appear to those of the nonpsychic world, this is my recollection."

Don speaks now of avatars, who, he explains, are embodiments or incarnations of angels, who reside in heaven and serve as counselors to God. "I was one of these counselors with no thought of doing anything else or being anywhere else, other than what and where I was. Then God entered the celestial sphere to say, 'You are going to Earth. It is your task to communicate with humans and discern what you can of their psyche. You must learn about their emotions, including those which induce hatred to one another and when you return,' you must explain human anger and hatred to Me. You are sent to learn, but equally important, will be your report when you return." To this day, Don believes it is his unvarying, fundamental task to learn and to comprehend human behaviour, and despite how arduous and confounding the task, he is resolved to do this. It is his explanation for the distance he has travelled thus far in life both as a psychic and a man.

"God gave each one of us free will," he avows. "We can choose our pathway, either that of good or of evil. It is our choice. Free will," Don states, "is God's 'gift' to humans, for without it we are nothing but puppets." He ponders, however, how frequently it is we abuse this 'gift.' "How often," he questions, "do we mortals hurt, maim or even obliterate other human beings, and further, how frequently is it that we lie, steal, cheat, and carry out every other negative, grievous trait, known to mankind.

"It is difficult to fathom," he laments, "and yet, every day we witness the end result of human flaws and depravity." He passionately worries and laments that when he is called home again, his explanations to God will be difficult if not impossible, as he attempts to explain mankind's psyche, but he passionately believes this is his earthly task. It has been given to me by God," he affirms, "and because it is, I cannot, I must not fail in my duty."

QUESTION 6

What was your first experience in this field?

"It occurred when we lived in Toronto," he remembers, "When at age 13, I met a lady who lived next door. As it turned out, she had serious boyfriend issues and wanted my help to resolve the situation."

Don recollects, "My neighbour obviously detected my paranormal characteristics, and subsequently, bought me a set Tarot Cards, so I could read her situation. All she wanted to know was whether her boyfriend would resume their defunct relationship, but it turned out to be a far more complicated situation than initially thought to be, because I soon discovered she was actually a working occult specialist, so I immediately severed my relationship with her, although she protested because she felt I could help her.

I simply did not then and even today, will not involve myself with anyone connected with another paranormal sphere. I might consult occasionally with another sensitive, but I try never to interfere or intercede into another psychic's professional orbit, because I believe it would be an intrusion that is both invasive and confusing. It is something I will not do."

QUESTION 7

Do you envision things before, as, or after they happen, or all of the above?

Don responds immediately that his psychic ability functions fittingly in each of these categories, although he admits because it does, he will also receive information now and then he doesn't want to know. To corroborate this revelation, Don shares an old memory when a client came to his home, sat down at the kitchen table for a reading, when suddenly an overwhelming, negative sensation enveloped him. "I told her to go to the hospital immediately."

"But why?" she asked. "Because you are dying," I replied. She looked at me with shock and disbelief and said, "No, no, look at me, I feel fine, in fact, I feel perfectly well." But I warned her, "You are not well, you have no aura, and nothing that encircles you depicts well-being. I see only serious illness."

The lady, however, did not go to the hospital. She did not take Don's advice, and as he sadly recalls this incident, he laments two weeks later she did pass away. To this day he believes had she listened to his warning, she would have been protected and lived, and concludes people will often think they are healthy and all is well with them when often it is not. "Changes can occur quickly," he cautions, "so be grateful for good health, but also be prepared for sudden variations that come without warning. Each one of us, by paying close attention, can detect harmful variations in our health early enough to seek medical care."

QUESTION 8

Have you ever been incorrect in your readings?

Don carefully ponders this question before he replies, but when he does, there is no hesitancy in his voice. "No, not that I know of... well, perhaps with a time line as to when something will happen, then I may have been occasionally inaccurate. But the answer is no, too, because I haven't been wrong in my actual predictions."

He cautions, however, if people knew every answer to every question all of the time, we would exist in God's throne room and not live here on earth. Don believes God is the only One who has all the answers, the only One who can know or see all, or predict the future perfectly. God alone is omniscient, but Don asserts that often when God does speak to us, many of us do not hear His voice or heed His words. "Hindsight," he concludes, "is always 20/20 and frequently, the purpose of an event isn't always clear until after the fact, but I try carefully to use the psychic 'gift' He has given to me and in the most perfect way I can."

QUESTION 9

What, if any, was your worst, most scary or negative experience when using your 'gift?'

"How easily I can recall a lady who came to my house for a reading" he remembers, "when within seconds after she sat down I said, I cannot read you."

"What do you mean?" she asked. "What is wrong?"

I replied, "Your aura emits something evil and I can easily deduce that you practice black magic. You must leave now," and she did.

Don told her to leave because he was immediately aware of the harm she could do to him. "She had the power to evoke an evil spirit or entity that would in turn torment or drive me demoniacally. I knew instantly she must leave my home, but alas, the evil she did emit lingered for some time to come."

Speaking slowly, quietly, almost as if he were reliving the experience at the moment, Don said he instantly recognized the danger she presented, and further, he knew she had been sent by a demon, or he laments, "by the devil himself."

It is here he stops to explain a devil spirit, who in his circles is called, 'Top Hat Man.'

"His home covers the world over, and he is a dangerous, destructive spirit that every psychic must avoid at all costs." Don's relief is palatable as he completes this portion of his story, but he then relates yet another negative incident that involved a woman in Toronto. He was very young, he recalls, but this person set him on a course which would end with the temporary loss of his psychic/medium abilities.

"This lady," he remembers, "was of Greek heritage, and as soon as she entered my home, she placed one thousand dollars cash on the kitchen table, and asked me to place a spell on her son, so that he would not marry a woman that she deemed unsuitable.

"Foolishly, avariciously, and ashamedly, I used my paranormal power to comply, when almost immediately my psychic abilities vanished. Simultaneously, I was instantly aware that every worthwhile aspect of my life would change. I lost my job, my apartment, every component of my life as it was then, vanished. I had abused my powers and the Spirit Guides were extremely angry and disappointed in what I had done. My 'gift' vanished and as it did, I was to learn a bitter lesson, and one it seems I had to learn the hard way. It was a desolate time." Don relates he was forced to leave Toronto, move back to St. John's, Newfoundland, and once there, forced to live on the streets for three weeks where he was lost, lonely, devastated, and uncertain where life would lead him. Don felt trapped in misery and confusion, and despite his constant and earnest prayers, help did not arrive and there was nothing to extract him from this abyss, until suddenly about three weeks after his move back home, the penalty was lifted and he was allowed to begin again. "I learned my lesson," he concedes, "how I learned my lesson."

Don declares emphatically, "It was a lesson never to be forgotten, and I am still today grateful I could resume my psychic life, marry and live each day exhilarated and engaged in my 'gifted' field." His addendum to this story, however, is that his powers did block the marriage as requested by the Greek lady, but in doing this Don's life was forever altered. Later in his story, Don has agreed to discuss the rule by which psychic mediums are supposed to live, and although he once exploited these regulations in his psychic life, it will never happen again.

QUESTION 10

Do you have a favourite or most memorable client-based session?

"Yes," Don affirms, "but it is not a happy memory. It concerns the lady I advised to go to the hospital but who would not. It troubled me that she could have saved her life but would not, and my lesson was and is that although I can help people to consider positive decisions, I cannot force them to do so. All I can do is issue a warning, a suggestion, a heads-up, but the rest is up to the individual, for whom I am reading."

QUESTION 11

How do you acquire your clients?

Without hesitation, Don exclaims . . . "Word of mouth. Only word of mouth. I do not have a website, nor do I advertise, all my clients come to me by word of mouth from others, who are satisfied and happy with my readings or I assume they must be. However, in one's psychic life, we may not hear from clients who are gratified and happy, although others will surface occasionally especially if they have a need to blame others for their bad fortune. They can be rude and complaintive, but to be honest," exclaims a grateful Don, "I seldom have anyone complain about my readings and I am grateful because it is my purpose to help not hinder my clients."

QUESTION 12

Can you as a psychic manipulate a person for whom you are doing a reading?

"I cannot, but another psychic might be tempted to do this through black magic but that is another story all together." Don believes, "God forbids this fabricated use of His 'gift,' and accordingly for me, I strive never to misuse my paranormal 'gift.' There are, however, unscrupulous psychics," he laments, "who do not practice with a transparent sense of right and wrong, and will and sometimes do exploit their paranormal powers in a harmful way."

How do they do this?

"Well, for instance," Don relates "there are documented cases wherein a client might want something to happen so profoundly in life, and then verbalize this desire with a psychic, who may then advise that should the client ante up an additional and usually large amount of money. The psychic will then use his advanced paranormal powers to make that something happen."

There is obvious anger in his voice when he states this misapplication occurs all too frequently, but Don is adamant it is a despicable use of God's 'gift,' to say nothing of the negative impact it has on the client. He cautions would be clients to be circumspect and careful in their choice of a psychic, and should such a circumstance develop, leave immediately.

QUESTION 13

Is there ever a time or with a certain kind of person, where your 'gift' does not work, and if so, why is this?

"Yes," Don responds, "several times such phenomena has occurred in a session and each time it involved people who were incredibly arrogant and so ostensibly in control of everything in their lives or tried to be that my psyche could not break through. I must admit though," he continues, "in order to read these clients, I have resorted to the use of strong paranormal authority, and because it is the only way to ensure a client will comprehend the obstruction we face is, in reality, a result of his own behaviour. If a client projects a self-important, arrogant attitude, it can block my ability to execute a reading," he concludes, "and I am grateful it does not occur too often in my psychic work. Still, I admit it can happen."

QUESTION 14

Do you control your psychic power or does it have authority over you?

"It has dominance over me," Don states emphatically, "but I must give permission for it to have that authority. Sometimes it manifests so loudly and intrusively that I must command it to leave, but I never want it to completely depart, because it is so much a part of who I am and who I will always be."

Don's tried and true method to exercise control over his psyche, is to watch scary, horror movies, the more frightening the better, because they relax him. "I know the stories are not real, they are farfetched, and they are make-believe, but they soothe me, help me to fall asleep, and essentially, desensitize me, which is the exact opposite of how they would affect most other people," he contends.

QUESTION 15

Do you consider your psychic power a 'gift' or a 'curse?'

Without hesitation, Don replies, "it is a 'gift,' a 'gift' from God, and although I am humbled I also feel somewhat special too, because surely God will only bestowed so exceptional a 'gift' if one is considered trustworthy and sufficiently special to carry through and help others. I know God has entrusted me with this 'gift' but only to serve and help others."

One does not doubt that Don sincerely believes the origin of his 'gift' because his voice conveys conviction that repulses skepticism. He cares not what others think because his life as a psychic originates from God, and only it is through God that Don believes he can continue his work.

QUESTION 16

Do you have to summon the 'gift' or does it have a will of its own?

"It is present all the time, every day of my life, but for me to hear, to grasp the message it conveys, I must be grounded and connected to my emotions. If I am unhappy, which I seldom am, it can block. I have everything a human requires to be happy. I am a simple man. I do not live in an ostentatious house, but my modest home is much more than those who are poor and have no home. Happiness does not emanate from material possessions," he believes, "it comes from the peace and satisfaction within us."

QUESTION 17

How do strangers react when you encounter them? Do they have any idea or realization that you have the 'gift?'

"When I do meet people, especially strangers who do not know me or what I do, they will often draw near to me out of nowhere and begin to chat. They find me approachable and easy to confide in, although they will acknowledge we have never met. I remember an incident that occurred outside of a Walmart in my city, when I went outside for a smoke.

"A person I didn't know came over to chat, but instantly I recognized from his aura he was troubled and needed to talk, and he then proceeded to relate several issues of concern to him. I proposed several possible solutions, after which he thanked me and left. Although he didn't know I am a psychic, he did mention for some reason he felt inexplicably drawn to me, and following that hasty encounter, he seemed to be more comfortable, relaxed, and perhaps more prepared to confront his difficulties. Remember," Don declares, "this encounter was unplanned and extemporaneous, for he was a stranger, a person with unresolved issues, but he was also a man who felt I may have some answers for him, or at the very least I was a person with whom he could chat for a few minutes. This phenomenon actually does occur time and again," he concludes, "but I simply consider such incidents as a reflection of the 'gift.'

QUESTION 18

Once people are alerted that you are gifted, that you have psychic powers, do they react with:

Skepticism?

Fear?

Disbelief?

Of the three choices, Don does not hesitate to reveal that clients will often mention their disbelief, not so much in him but rather in his ability to relate factual aspects of their lives about which he had no foreknowledge. "Believe me," he laughs, "I have heard it all, and I am asked how do you do this? How can you be so accurate with the information you impart and although I frequently try to explain, it simply doesn't register?"

QUESTION 19

Do your psychic powers ever get you into trouble?

"Oh yes," and he again refers to the incident in Toronto when he cast a spell that got him into serious trouble. "It was a lesson learned the hard way," states Don, "but I have also discovered many of my clients may already perceive what I am about to tell them regarding their lives, although they may not admit it. I simply reaffirm and never camouflage or prevaricate because falsehood and misinterpretation both have a way of catching up to destroy credibility."

It is now Don specifically mentions various well-known psychics for whom he has total contempt. They prey on the sad, the lonely, the bereaved, and they do it strictly for money. "Their ploy is obvious," he laments. "It is a case of pay more and more and I will foretell more about and for you." Don calls it a vile ruse, and advises if this happens in a reading, "leave."

It is obvious, although he will not divulge names, that Don believes his profession is one for the most part, populated by credible and trustworthy psychics, but it is also rife with dishonor and disreputable practitioners, for whom he has no patience or empathy. "We are not given this 'gift' to abuse it or to take advantage of those who need our guidance." When this occurs, it is a travesty and painful for him to acknowledge.

"There is nothing I can do about it but issue a warning," he concludes.

QUESTION 20

Do doors that would normally be difficult to enter, open for you because of your psychic powers?

He declares an emphatic 'no!'

"I will never abuse my 'gift' by using it to such a purpose, to establish relationships, or for personal gain." Don reveals he has no interest in meeting 'personalities' whether they are rock stars, politicians, Hollywood stars, or anyone in public life. "As far as I am concerned," he states, "we are all equal in God's view, wherein money and position have no preference or importance."

At this point in the interview, the writer hears vociferous barking in the background, and asks Don if he has a dog? The joyous inflection that permeates his voice when he replies is palatable. "Oh yes, it is our little Chihuahua, who has three beds, is dreadfully spoiled and equally demanding of my time and my love." Don then explains animals have their own heavenly protector, St. Francis of Assisi, Patron Saint of Animals, however, after listening to him extol about the pampered daily life of his pet, one can scarcely believe this pup will have little need of St. Francis; certainly not as long as he has Don in his life.

QUESTION 21

Are you a healer, and is a healer different from a medium?

"Yes, they are different," Don advises, "however, I can be both if I chose to be." He explains, "If a client would come to me for a diagnosis, I am able to tell or advise him to seek medical treatment. Incredibly I can feel and frequently ascertain in advance if one has a health problem," and recounts a situation when his insight undoubtedly saved his client's life.

"She was an older lady," he remembers, "and immediately upon meeting her, I knew she had a serious health problem. I told her to get a mammogram immediately, and although she questioned my advice, she did try to arrange an immediate examination at a nearby facility. The waiting list was long, and appointments were months away, so I then urged her to find another clinic, even one that might be a great distance from her home. At the clinic, she was immediately diagnosed with advanced but still treatable, breast cancer. Today," Don utters with relief, "this lady is now well and lives a full and healthy life.

QUESTION 22

How do you control this gift or does it need to be controlled?

"To be honest," Don admits, "my paranormal psyche can emerge at times without notice," which he corroborates by sharing this event. "It concerns my partner's friend, a coworker who had recently lost her father. She was in deep mourning when we met, but almost instantly her dad appeared to me, and asked me to convey a message as to how dearly he loved and missed her. The revelation brought tears, but it always gave her heart ease and joy, and this was a certainly a time when my compulsion to reveal a psychic revelation, did supersede my control.

"But most times when it is required," Don says, "I do have control and I will walk away from a situation, although I admit my conviction to do this doesn't always work. There are certainly other times when a situation will materialize and my psyche compels me to blurt out what I see."

QUESTION 23

Is psychic power the same as intuitive power?

"They are of the same family," Don believes, "similar as is penicillin is to amoxicillin. They are different, and yet, they have a similar purpose, but do not necessarily tender the same effect. Psychic power requires feelings, a reaction to emotions, while intuitive power is more about how one interprets facial expressions and physical movements." Don practices both in his work.

QUESTION 24

Can these 'gifts' be misused?

"Oh yes, they can," exclaims Don, and offers this example. "A bereaved client may visit a psychic medium with the hope he can make contact with a loved one who has passed, only to have that same psychic claim for an astronomical sum (especially if he knows the client has the means) he will initiate the link. But the proviso is predicated on the reprehensible request for exorbitant remuneration.

"This so-called psychic," Don laments, "is a charlatan, whose blatant misuse of the 'gift' is appalling and he will be marked as one who preys on sadness and bereavement, both of which are forbidden in the rules." Those rules, he concludes, are simple: "a psychic must be highly principled and show love to all."

QUESTION 25

Is it possible for one with the 'gift' to become arrogant in having it?

"Yes" Don emphatically admits, "a psychic who has forfeited humility and forgotten the origin of his paranormal powers can easily become self-important and over-confident. This is why each one of us must constantly remind ourselves that we are only the channel for God's purpose and we are not here to bolster our own ego or reward."

QUESTION 26

Because you believe your 'gift' comes from God, can it be purloined by the devil or evil forces?

"Not stolen," Don replies, "but manipulated." He gives this explanation. "Say, for example, I want to purchase a new car, regularly save for it by working long hours, put aside the money, only to find it is urgently needed elsewhere. Nefarious forces might encourage me to make a wrong decision as to where the funds should go, or might entice me to steal or commit a crime, so I can get that new vehicle immediately.

"The consequences," Don advises, "can be negative and catastrophic. I strive to carefully ensure evil forces do not influence my work, nor sanction misuse of my paranormal 'gift.' I do not use it for self-gain or gratification, and I try to keep my guard up to resist when temptation knocks which it does now and then."

QUESTION 27

Fanciful as it might be, what is Heaven like as envisioned by a psychic?

Once again, Don, who is deeply religious, readily and happily discusses his faith. He believes every human being now alive or yet to be born, is initially domiciled in heaven and will be there until God deems it is time to leave. "Here," he declares, "there is a book in which every person's name is inscribed on its pages, in bold black ink. It is a huge book, greyish in colour, 20 feet by 20 feet or more," he asserts, "and it is so wide one cannot imagine its size."

Don reveals when he tried to touch it, it began to move and shake on its own, as though to indicate 'do not touch.'

"However," he recalls, "the admonition was not severe but more akin to a parent telling a child 'no' in a gentle, non-aggressive way. I am certain this was done not to instill fear or dread, but rather to affirm this 'book of life' is inaccessible to mortals and for me, this is an image that will be forever etched in my mind." Don switches topics to discuss his very real concept of Heaven and what, he maintains, each one of us will encounter, once we are there. "Heaven," he believes, "is God's palace. It is his home and it is beautiful and peaceful. There is no pain, no suffering, no anger, and no animosity. There is only boundless tranquility and love.

"There," he continues, "you will find only beauty where celestial houses and shops dot the streets, and stunning carriages drawn by exquisite horses, make their way down perfect roads. It is a place where those who have passed will find sweet serenity and happiness on every street and in every home." Don queries, "why anyone would fear death? Can we have a more perfect home? Heaven is as real to me as is life here on earth and when it is my time to pass away; I will be more than ready to live there."

Don has this vision of heaven because he has been there. "I have travelled through the tunnel, not as a deceased body, but as a living human being and I heartily confirm God and his counsel dwell in a palace with many rooms, where goodness and light ensure happiness for all who deserve and have earned their place there. However," he also advises, "it is here also where God will judge the quick and the dead, as depicted in the Bible." Don reveals we will see God, seated on His throne in a room with a pool that offers the unborn four choices and because it is mandatory to select one, there is also a spirit guide to help.

The choices, according to Don are:
1. To be poor and homeless.
2. To be wealthy with every material advantage.
3. To be humble and middle class.
4. To be humble and poor but righteous.

There is a catch; Don reveals "because every person tempted to choose wealth with every luxury is denied the opportunity to learn the important lessons in life. On the other hand, if one selects another of the choices, he is assured these same great lessons will be absorbed and the rewards will be considerable, when we return to heaven to an elevation beyond imagination." Don cautions as simple as it might seem, the choices are not without peril, and cautions all to remember, "It is God and He alone, who will ultimately render the final decision as to our fate. This he will do for reasons that are His alone to know."

QUESTION 28

How many hours a week do your use your paranormal powers?

"Every day of my life. I generally work ten to twelve hours daily. I never shut down or close up and my client base stretches from here to Alberta and British Columbia, and beyond. I use Skype to connect with clients, although I don't have to see them or have them see me to enact a reading. My Spirit Guide pilots me through each encounter, which is why I am so certain my clients are satisfied with their readings."

QUESTION 29

Does a psychic believe or know?

"To know is indisputable true fact," Don declares. "To believe is based on faith, trust and a connection with the Almighty." He reveals when he is outside a building, he will sense immediately if rain is coming and often anticipates other major changes in nature, long before they occur. This statement then reminds Don of God's promise to never again flood the earth as recorded in Noah's story, and as affirmation of His word, created the rainbow for mankind, as proof of his covenant.

QUESTION 30

Is it true a psychic because of his intuitive abilities, will have no fear of dying because of his knowledge regarding the other side?

"Every psychic should have no fear of death if he possesses true paranormal powers. He will know what to expect, and will acknowledge there is nothing to fear. Each one of us will receive all God has promised, once heaven becomes our everlasting home."

QUESTION 31

Is life for a psychic more tranquil, less stressful, and more meaningful, because of the 'gift?'

Don's reply as has no other in his narrative, is shocking, for surely every day is blessed and filled with excitement and challenge, if you possess paranormal powers. However, he maintains, "Life as a psychic is boring."

The next question. How can this be?

Reply, "Because we know what is ahead, what has happened in the past, the cause and effect of each and there are seldom surprises." Don hears the incredulity in my reaction and quickly adds he is personally at peace, so the mundane aspects of his work are wholly acceptable.

QUESTION 32

Do clients ever become angry or frustrated with the information gleaned from your readings?

"Oh yes, they certainly do," Don admits, and it is now following the many hours he has spent discussing his career, when he admits that all his clients are not pleasant, courteous people. "Many of them become extremely upset and acrimonious," he vents, "and do not hesitate to tell me so. When this occurs," he continues, "I simply remind them they may be to blame if, for instance, they have not been truthful with me. I remind them it is their life I see, not mine. I am only the messenger; however, honest, open dialogue is necessary, if I am to ensure a fruitful reading."

Don refers to a reading which occurred the day previous, when a client wanted to discuss her marriage. As she revealed facts and incidents an immense revelation came to Don, who said, "You are involved with another person. Beware, because this illicit liaison will destroy your marriage." This obviously upset the client, but he continued, "Your husband is still unaware of your affair but he soon will be, so the next move is up to you. The client left both shocked and perplexed as to how I knew what I did, but it may be she might give serious thought to the jeopardy her actions had created in her life. I am not judgmental," he says, "that is not my job, but I must reveal my visions as they appear to me. If this upsets the client, who may try to deny the information, there is no doubt we both know the truth. But what, if anything is done with the information revealed during a reading, is entirely up to the client."

QUESTION 33

Who are your clients, not by name but what profession, background are they from?

"They come from every background, every profession, in province, out of province, out of country, and others who are closer to home. As mentioned, I do not advertise but the clients keep coming."

QUESTION 34

Do you, or have you ever seen a spirit, an angel or any such entity in your work?

"Absolutely," Don replies, "although I try to control the 'gift' it does have a will of its own, so I see spirits, even demons, every single day. In order to put my mind at rest, I constantly prepare myself for their appearance and enlist my psychic self to protect me."

QUESTION 35

Given how hard you work in a given day, do you have any fear of burning out?

"I am involved in my psychic work nine to ten hours every day as mentioned and some days are even longer. Because Skype permits sessions to occur with clients in Alberta, British Columbia and elsewhere, it is true my hours are erratic and scattered because of the time change. Burnout will never happen because I love what I do, which means I can relax and decompress when I am not at work."

QUESTION 36

If you foresee illness or death, will you discuss these revelations with a client? If not, what if your disclosure would encourage a client to seek medical help and may then become well? Or, what if you could change the course of an accident or injury to a person, would this embolden you to speak out?

"I will and generally I do," Don reveals, "but I have learned although there are clients who will react positively, they are others who simply cannot. For instance, if I foresee illness and advise a client to see a doctor, as happened with the lady mentioned earlier, some clients will heed my advice but others in the same situation will not. I am a messenger. I can do no more than encourage my clients."

Don sadly admits he has clients who will actually hurt themselves and are suicidal, but fail in the effort to take their own lives. When they ultimately seek his counsel, he is pragmatic and honest. "I remember a client whose beloved grandson suffered from schizophrenia and in this tormented state he did not want to live. As seemingly harsh and extraordinary his advice was, he told his client her boy simply wanted to go 'home' and further, his potential demise was perhaps the best choice for him."

It appears in his psychic work; Don McGrath is a realist, no matter how difficult the subject may be.

REFERENCES

PSYCHIC DON MCGRATH
REFERENCE GINA ELENS
NEWFOUNDLAND, CANADA

There was no doubt in her mind when Gina Elens realized she was in desperate need of help in her life and then came to realize the assistance she required must come from a psychic. She did maintain a trusted friendship with psychic acquaintances the world over, but Gina wanted to connect with a psychic she could meet face to face. Further, it had to be someone she did not know.

"I was going through the worst time in my life," Gina freely admits, "so help and precise interpretation to these events was seriously essential." To keep her initial appointment with Don, she had to drive through the worst snowstorm of the year but the greatest ordeal was yet to come. "I walked into our first meeting when only minutes later, Don informed me he could not help me with certain events because I had someone else with whom I was communicating. I admit I was confused and thought him to be a nut, but I was there determined to discover what he knew about my circumstances." What occurred next was amazing, as Don described this person right down to appearance, where her family lived and other pertinent details about their relationship. "He was absolutely correct as he portrayed my friend/teacher/psychic, but I was dumbfounded, although I knew instantly the relationship with her was over and Don was now the counsellor I needed." Gina admits, as they sat down at the beginning of the session, she did not want to hear what Don would say. "Remember," she admits, "the truth is sometimes hard to take in and difficult to bear."

Don did not hesitate to go straight to the heart of Gina's problems and was quick to warn her that pain, hurt and distress lies ahead and must be immediately confronted. He also advised she must develop patience, faith and absolute trust in herself, because her future would then be all she wanted it to be. "I must believe in me," Don advised, "and I must pay attention to the teachings of Spirit, and strive to restrain and restrict the negative energy or it would consume me." Finally, in that first session, Don counselled Gina if her determination and resolve were strong, her struggles would dissolve and she would be free. Gina knows many people who have sought the psychic counsel of Donald McGrath, and each person has conveyed to her his accuracy in defining their lives and further expressed how his 'gift' helped them. "What can I say about Donald?" Without hesitation she exclaims, "He is an amazing psychic, medium, healer and teacher, not just to me but to many others. He is my friend more like family and from personal experience; I know he has saved many lives."

Because of Don, Gina believes her life is now functional because he cares. "He is blessed by God and he has become an essential part of my life. I cannot remember life before Don and I believe fate or karma brought us together. He is the best at what he does and his revelations are honest and true."

Because of the psychic's intervention in her life and his advice, she developed personal patience and enhanced her faith. It was then her life improved, and Gina steadfastly believes because she listened to Don all those years ago, "I am alive, my family is happy and life is good. To thank him seems trivial, when it comes to describing what he has done for me, my spirit and my family." Gina is convinced the continued presence of Don McGrath in her life will ensure she enjoys blessings beyond description.

PSYCHIC DON MCGRATH
REFERENCE AMANDA HARRIGAN
ST. JOHN'S, NEWFOUNDLAND
CANADA

Following her disappointment with two or three previous psychic readings, Amanda Harrigan might well have given up her search for a qualified psychic who would reveal specific, pertinent information she wanted, but then she met Don McGrath and her quest was finally over. "Those previous sessions were completely generic," she remembers, "with comments such as, 'you will take a trip' or 'in your future there are keys to a new vehicle or house,' or other banal predictions applicable to anyone at all.

"I was always intrigued with psychic readers, who could foresee events into the future, but I also longed to meet a psychic with whom I would find rapport but it was equally important to me, he would be someone willing to discuss the afterlife. My search seemed in vain until I met Don, who is both specific and detailed in his interpretation of every paranormal domain.

"I learned about Don from a trusted friend, who was extremely impressed with him, when in her sessions he revealed precise details about her family members, some of whom had passed away. He also accurately described people who were present in her daily life, and my friend was awestruck when he perfectly described their specific characteristics and personalities, so referral to me was made easy."

Because Amanda was determined to maintain an open mind, she resolved to postpone any opinion until after the reading and felt no apprehension or hesitation when she finally met with Don. "I was fully prepared to give him the benefit of any lingering doubt or misgivings which were leftovers from previous readings, but it was a profound pleasure to discover he was a 'gifted' and caring man. His care and interest in helping clients are immediately apparent, and his demeanour and actions ensure one is instantly comfortable with him."

She describes Don as 'laid back' with a talent to lighten the mood and make one believe almost immediately you have known each other for years. "He is easy to speak to and allows a client to ask questions throughout the reading. It is obvious he thoroughly enjoys what he does but what impressed me most is his dedicated purpose to ensure a client will leave with information pertinent to his or her needs."

Amanda finds his readings accurate with detail and correct information about her past, current and future circumstances. "Amazingly," she reveals, "he actually described the various personalities presently involved in my life and precisely portrayed their lives. Because I was going through a confusing time when we met, I needed guidance and reassurance in my personal life.

"Now, three years later, I unequivocally confirm Don's readings are not only accurate but reflect a truth when the truth is something you would rather not know." Amanda ruefully reveals she was in an unstable marriage and involved with another man, when she first met with Don. "Although it seemed life with this person was where I needed to be, I was also confused and unsure as to what path to take. I was uncertain he was equally committed to me and I was concerned about his honesty."

As Amanda continued to see Don, he quickly confirmed the man was not only dishonest but was actually involved with another woman during the time they were together. Then, as Don described this man's actions to a tee, she was amazed when he actually provided cogent details regarding the 'other woman.' Don warned this guy would continue to pursue her in an effort to prolong the relationship, and he was again proved correct. Amanda found it surprising when the psychic accurately detailed the man's inner fears and feelings, all of which she was woefully familiar.

Amanda concludes her assessment of psychic, Don, by declaring without his counsel and guidance, she has no idea where her life would be. "His advice is invaluable to me even now, as daily I forge ahead in this uncertain world."

PSYCHIC DON MCGRATH
REFERENCE LUNA
MAURITIUS, INDIA

Luna and Don met two years ago after a friend introduced them, however, they did not meet in person or by telephone, but rather over Skype. "I was going through a harrowing personal time and needed help which until then, was elusive. Immediately following our initial session and because of Don, I underwent a life-altering experience and embarked on my journey back to a life that encouraged purpose and offered serenity.

"I will never forget those initial moments with Don when his first words were: "I can see someone behind you. Don't move!" Luna admits she completely 'freaked out' when the psychic perfectly described her uncle, who had committed suicide in 1993. She firmly believes this uncle had been sent by her family to cause her harm and despite incredulity, offers this explanation.

"I am the eldest grandchild in a family where my parents, through hard work, developed a successful logistics company and gained great wealth. Obtaining an education was not an option for me or my brothers. It was expected. I have two Master's degrees, one of my brothers is a doctor and I have another brother presently in Singapore, completing his Bachelor's Degree in International Business." And yet, despite the sterling opportunities given to her family, Luna reveals envy, jealousy and selfish motives were prevalent and it is within this environment Luna believes her grandmother and aunts entreated her dead uncle's spirit to harm her and disrupt her life. This done in part because of her intellect and supreme ambition to be the best she can be in her life. But because she often functions outside the mores of her culture, it is obvious her traditional relatives are displeased. Luna is reluctant to reveal too many details regarding her family situation because they would be the source of further issues, but she is adamant a dead uncle had invaded her life.

"When Don commanded the spirit to leave, it did," she recalls, "after which the psychic also revealed facts and specific details regarding my life. They were mostly negative and affected every aspect of my day to day existence." Although Luna was assured of Don psychic skills by a trusted friend, she nonetheless, found it difficult initially to believe he could help her. There just seemed so much that was awry in her life. In her desperate state, Luna resolved to follow Don's advice; no matter how extraordinary it might be, the first of which entreated her to perform certain rituals guaranteed to remove the negative environment which surrounded her. Peculiar as it seemed, she followed his instructions and after the first session and over the next three days, she obediently lit three white candles, showered with salt water and oranges, kept salt in the corners of the house, placed light sage and used smoke to clean the entire property, all of which was done to ensure her uncle could not enter her personal space.

"Esoteric as this might seem to others," Luna declares, "for me it was a cleansing process which eventually allowed me to sleep through the night free of frightening nightmares which had permeated my every attempt."

Don also advised Luna during those early sessions to monitor her sleep patterns for several days which she did. Today she is unequivocally convinced his intervention eradicated her uncle's presence and allowed her to resume a positive and carefree life. Following the cleansing ritual and even to present day, Luna admits, "If a negative thought invades my mind, I light a candle and it works. There is a part of me that believes if one has faith, one will find light. For me, Don is the source of that light." When Don was recovering from serious surgery, Luna worried her frequent calls would interrupt his convalescence but her need for his intercession was essential. "I didn't want to be selfish but I needed him, and although Don does protect himself, we were mutually concerned he may be negatively affected following the removed of my uncle's spirit. There were other family issues which also required resolution, and although I tried to give him time to recover, it is true early on, my contact with him was frequent."

Stress is a tremendous motivator, Luna opines, and admits her situation was the source of a depression so severe she frequently felt the only way out was to end her life. Don changed everything for her and even now remains her guide. "He has never refused to come to my aid, and is a wonderful person with whom

I can speak freely. I admit there are times when our chats seem to be about nothing in particular, but then again they can be about absolutely everything."

Despite distance and Skype as their only means of contact, Luna finds Don to be a patient and loving person and one who tries his best to respond to a client's needs. He does not cushion his advice, but Luna knows in her heart, his concern for her is real. "When he blesses and wishes me a happy life at the conclusion of our sessions, they are my talismans until our next communication."

A FINAL NOTE

My interview time with Don concludes and when I mention this to him, his response is surprising and unexpected. "I am relieved and happy to see this month end," he declares. "It has been an unhappy time for everyone as there is harmful energy everywhere.

"I have had the strangest clients all this past week," Don reveals, "indeed many more than usual, including those with alcohol and drug addictions, others, who have serious marital problems, those who are suffering with mental illness or changes occurring in their lives with which they cannot cope, and then, there are others who feel lonely and shunned by society.

"I do not judge," he reaffirms, "but it is difficult to understand why people hurt themselves, why they are often their own worst enemy which they often are. I 'see' all this, as I struggle to resolve endless problems with and for them. It is why God has blessed me with the 'gift' and these problems are why I will, every day of my life, continue to help others when possible." Don finally underscores one more time, in the most devout voice one can hear, "It is by God, through God and because of God, many of my clients today live more peaceful lives. It is solely because the Lord bestowed this 'gift' to me, and it is my life long duty, to use it wisely and sensibly." There is one overriding crystal clear fact I have learned about Don. He loves his job, his clients, his life, his partner, his mother and his dog. Here is a man content with the simple comforts in life, and questions if those who live in luxurious homes or have every extravagance in life, are any happier than he is. It is doubtful they can be because as he shares more and more of his personality and character, one is certain Don is intensely honest, genuine and sincerely values his more humble position in life.

He seems to want no more than what he currently has and is more concerned about the comfort and happiness of those he loves than his own status. When you connect with Don, when you hear his voice, when you witness his determination to serve his clients honestly and truthfully as a psychic, you cannot deny he is sincere. He actually said, "I live in a trailer but it is a place where respect and love abide." He also looks after his mother, who lives in a separate accommodation on his property, and with whom I had the privilege to share a conversation.

She does not claim to fully understand what Don does or how he does it, but there is no doubt she is one of his greatest supporters. For the mother of Don McGrath, there is no question he is the "Best son ever and I am the one who is blessed." For those who have read Don's story and might like to make contact or acquire further information, you can reach him:

Telephone number:
709.739.9785
email: dudeman4you_98@yahoo.com
His fees are:
$30.00 per psychic reading
$55.00 per medium session

Other paranormal service charges, such as the removal of negativity or evil from a home, are determined case by case.

PSYCHIC

DWAYNE SCULLION
RED DEER, ALBERTA
CANADA

AUTHOR'S NOTES

The instant Dwayne Scullion entered the room, I was struck by his youthful appearance, mature demeanour, his obvious self-assurance in what he does and following our chat, there was no denying he has undeniable confidence in himself. It was a surprise to learn this young man is 24 years of age and yet, he is so utterly convinced his sole purpose is to use his 'gift' to help others but on his terms, with no interference from anyone else.

You cannot judge a book by its cover the old adage advises and you certainly better not judge Dwayne by his age, although this is difficult because his appearance is youthful, his language is very much the vernacular of his generation and his enthusiasm is appealing and contagious, as found in the young.

Dwayne came to my attention several times before I decided to pursue him as a subject for the book, but it was certainly because of the accolades about his readings mentioned to me over time by several people I had never met and who did not know each other, but had heard about this book, ergo; I certainly became intrigued to learn more about him for myself.

In my many years as a writer, it was a first to contact a subject time and time again but receive no response, to the point I decided enough was enough and would terminate the effort. Then my innate, tenacious personality kicked in to dictate I must meet Dwayne to determine if he would be an interesting psychic for the book, so I tried again and immediately after that first conversation all doubt vanished. I knew he was.

Dwayne's story is considerably dissimilar from the lives of the other featured psychics, although it is a narrative worth telling because it is dissimilar, set apart and quite phenomenal, given Dwayne's tender years. During our first meeting my thoughts wandered to consider if my life might have been less challenging had I, at such a young age, possessed the assurance and confidence Dwayne has in himself.

Here is a warning, Dear Reader. Do not judge this psychic by his age, because he is successful, accomplished, has a waiting list of more than 300 people who want access to his talent and he is undeniably independent. One might assume this independence manifests itself in Dwayne either as arrogance or an uncaring attitude, but it does not. He cares a great deal about his clients, but he practices his profession on his terms and admits the bitter blows which severely wounded him in the past, now serve only to strengthen his belief in himself. Dwayne exudes high energy and is critical of other psychics if they are incompetent, insincere or 'read' only for money.

He will frequently secure readings for himself with other psychics, most of whom he vents, are often far off the mark when it comes to his life, however, he curtails his criticism. Rather, he politely challenges their readings as inaccurate, irrelevant and quickly leaves. Conversely, he does respect those psychics, who are accurate when they describe his character, personality and foretell plausible details, regarding his past and future.

Dwayne minces no words when he reveals other psychics often do not like him, have been unkind to him and frequently belittle him, because of his age. He doesn't care and it doesn't bother him because there is one factor clearly evident when you meet him. He is his own man today, tomorrow and forever, and his journey to present day has been difficult for him, strewn with loss and sadness, but despite the hardships he believes he has been strengthened by adversity. His resolve ensures he is content as to who he is and he is absolutely certain where he is, where he is going and how he will get there. On the day we met, Dwayne had resigned from his other career as a sports therapist, to concentrate solely on his paranormal profession. His unique business card reads, "It's Good to Know Somebody Who Knows . . ." which bolsters how certain he is of his 'gift.'

Obviously, I am struck by Dwayne's singular belief in himself and his unconditional commitment to follow his 'gift' wherever it will lead. He is in charge and where he goes his 'gift' will follow. Equally certain is his preparedness for the future, as he is obviously dedicated to do whatever is required to ensure he will always and forever, function in the esoteric world of the psychic/medium.

MEET DWAYNE SCULLION
PSYCHIC
SYLVAN LAKE, ALBERTA

At the tender age of 12 to 13, Dwayne Scullion knew he was different. He would envision details about people in his presence, but he also knew it was more prudent to say nothing and keep his revelations to himself. He did try but the images would not leave. They stayed with him everywhere and each time he met someone, anyone, the visions kept coming.

Irrespective of the constant prescience, it wasn't until he was 15 or so that he began to display his 'gift' and would stand on the corner in his hometown and literally 'read' for the graduating students from his school, or even for those people who would drive off the highway, to stop at the nearby service station. He could not help himself for Dwayne is a psychic and his 'gift' would no longer be ignored. "Other psychics believe," Dwayne states, "that every living person has the 'gift' of paranormal, the ability to learn or to be taught to 'read' others but I do not. I think this ability is a singular something that constitutes the psyche of a few and it is a trait that will not be ignored if you have it." Psychics are competitive, he admits and those who are truly paranormal do possess a self-subscribed knowledge about the others that is based on their persons' emotions, needs, and wants. Dwayne says a genuine psychic is one who possesses the ability to connect with a higher energy and concedes he does not know if the power comes from a Spirit Guide, but if you have it you know it. "Actually," he opines, "I have more than one and they are ever with me, always ready to assist when summoned.

"We are all connected to this spectral," he believes "but there are only a chosen few who can actually 'read' others. But when they do," Dwayne admonishes, "they had better remember why they have the 'gift,' where it comes from, and never abuse it."

"Love," he maintains, "is the basis of all that is good in life, and it is the common denominator when it comes to working with others in need of psychic help or empathy." It is here Dwayne reveals he is also a medium, and explains this is an entity that can connect with those who are no longer of this world. "To be a medium is exceedingly draining," he admits, "because it can be difficult to connect with those who have passed. I must unite with the very essence of their soul and when I do, although it is fundamental, it is also profoundly real." Dwayne will utilize Tarot cards to connect with the dead because initially they will assist him to first connect with his psychic self. Once accomplished, it is then the Spirit or Spirits, who advise, direct and help facilitate the initial contact and he is profoundly aware of their connection. To set the scene before a session, Dwayne will light a candle, more for ambience and atmosphere, but also because it calms and sets the scene for what is to come.

The client is situated in the meeting room when Dwayne enters to say "hello." Dwayne leaves the door slightly ajar because he is claustrophobic. He then discerns the aura of the person for whom he will be reading, but does not ask the person's name. If it is revealed, he tries to forget it because he wants to ensure this will be a generic session and not one connected specifically to the client until he begins.

"I do not focus on the past of the person with whom I am working," Dwayne says, "I am not judgemental nor am I offended or disturbed by what I learn. My Spirit Guide (and here again he states he is not convinced this is actually who it is there with him) will emerge and the session begins." With Spirit present, the counselling and revelations begin, and all that Dwayne sees and hears, he writes down to give to the client when the session ends. "Clients appreciate this gesture" he believes, "as it is something tangible as a reminder of the encounter.

"Often the client is nervous and reluctant to hear anything negative I might see," Dwayne admits, "but I relate what I see honestly and forthrightly, and believe to be forearmed is to be forewarned and I will not sugarcoat what I perceive to be the truth." He doesn't connect with the same Spirit at every reading, and admits he is never sure who might arrive from the Spirit world, but he is prepared to meet each one or all and articulates, he does respect each one.

Group 'readings' are out, although Dwayne has done them and he will not 'read' over the telephone. "The occasion is simply too personal, too private," he says, and adds, "what if I detect something my client may not want another to hear?" His clients must journey to his locale because he will not travel to meet them as he claims he is more comfortable and therefore, more precise in his own setting.

Dwayne lost three extremely close friends in the past few years and admitted the pain was almost unbearable. He has suffered just as everyone else does in a lifetime, but it is through distress and pain, both of which he says are synergetic to his work, that provide insight and strength to his psyche. Dwayne attempts to socialize with friends who respect his 'gift' and do not take advantage of his down time, but there are inevitable occasions when he will be approached by someone who will blatantly ask, "Are you that psychic I hear about?" and then immediately want to connect. "When this happens, I am polite, but also move on. I pretty much chill out at parties," he concedes, "but I might need a beer or two to do so. I have to come down, relax, and put aside the psychic thing." He counts on his friends to protect him but this doesn't always work, so he is keenly on guard in every circumstance. He also enjoys a wide range of music, the kind of which will depend on his mood, but for the most part he is a loner and one, who carefully maps his future, to control his leisure time as much as possible.

One factor seems absolutely certain. This young man, Dwayne Scullion, has his future well planned and completely charted, but the question is this: is Dwayne in charge or are his Spirits? He believes they are omnipresent to help ensure he does not stray from the future they require him to embrace? It is doubtful even Dwayne knows the answer to this question, unless those who perpetually occupy his paranormal sphere, choose to tell him.

DWAYNE'S PSYCHE ACTS OUT IN PUBLIC . . .

It is early Friday morning, Thanksgiving weekend, when Lisa calls to relate an incredible incident she had learned about the night before. Breathless, excited, eager to share because it involves Dwayne, whom she has never met, but opines I should know, because she is aware he is to be featured in this book. This is the same Lisa, who appears earlier in Don's story and she is absolutely correct because the story she recounts is compelling. But you, Dear Reader, will decide after you read this pertinent and crucial information as to whether it validates Lisa's call.

Lisa's dear friend has a young brother who subsists in a world beset with drugs, violence and dangerous people, and who will without compunction, hurt, seriously injure, or severely harm anyone who they believe has crossed, thwarted, or harmed their operation. One can imagine the pain and worry that assail the young man's family each and every time he leaves the house. Will it be to buy, to use, or perhaps, even to sell drugs for this nefarious group? They do not know, but this family is at the end of their endurance and they have no solutions to help their son, or conceivably save his life. This terrible burden besieges their lives day and night and despite their concerted effort, resolution remains elusive and discouraging. One day, the sister lunched at a fast food restaurant when a young man came in and walked over to the order desk. Still, it was obvious to her and extremely odd that he constantly looked her way and apparently wanted to approach her. But why, she wondered? As for the young man, all he could think of was how can he approach a person in a world where suspicion of strangers permeates society.

Uncertain that he should do so, but unable to control the impulse, Dwayne Scullion approached her, introduced himself as a local psychic, who had a message for her. He made reference to her brother and then revealed that her brother is in serious trouble involving drugs with a vile, repulsive, gang. He implored her to tell her brother if he does not get out immediately, within weeks at the most, he will be severely harmed.

One can imagine the shock and disbelief that shrouded the young lady, who had just been warned by a complete stranger of the paranormal world, about a situation within her family that has been kept secret and hidden from even the immediate family members. How could this be, she ponders? This is not Dwayne's first time to converse with a stranger because of those Spirits from beyond, who appear without warning, no matter where he is. Once they filter into his mind, he is compelled to act because if he does not, they persist until he does, and further, until he does, there is no respite from their intrusive possession.

There is another even more horrendous event which involves Dwayne, and occurred when he attended a social function for young people, who are happy and boisterous, as they are out to enjoy a good time. Before he arrives, he vows he will turn aside any psychic revelations that might emerge, so he can enjoy some down time and join in the fun. But moments after he enters the room, those inevitable Spirits descend without warning and Dwayne is compelled to seek out a young lady, who is standing in a group not far from him. The Spirits inform Dwayne this girl will be in serious trouble if she does not heed the advice he is to impart.

This introduction is more difficult because of the crowd, for after all this is a social occasion, and she is surrounded by friends and frivolity. But Dwayne interrupts her, introduces himself, explains what he does and then solemnly warns her, "You must end the relationship you are in with your present boyfriend, or you will be severely hurt by a knife which will leave you scarred." He employs all his skills to instill belief into this stunned young lady, who is shocked by the urgency of his warning, which is doubly disconcerting because it comes from someone she has never met and does not know. "Will she listen?" Dwayne wonders. "Will she follow my advice?" he repeatedly asks himself, and when she did contact him in a few days, he is devastated to learn she did not. The young lady is swathed in bandages, her face slashed by the dangerous boyfriend just as he predicted. Sadly, Dwayne is aware once again the Spirits have foretold an event he reluctantly revealed, so done because he knows these same Guides will not be denied. When they command him, it is apparent Dwayne has learned to obey.

THE EVOLUTION OF PSYCHIC

DWAYNE SCULLION
SYLVAN LAKE, ALBERTA

QUESTION 1

Are you a psychic medium?

"Yes, Dwayne replies, "I do consider myself a psychic and a medium, although to keep better control of these 'gifts' I don't offer both readings."

QUESTION 2

Is there a difference between a psychic and a psychic medium? Please define each one?

Dwayne quickly discloses his definitions are formulated from his limited psychic life, his personal views and his experiences. To him, there is a profound difference in the two spheres.

"When a client arrives for a reading," he conveys, "I ask if they know the difference between psychic work and mediumship, and if they don't, I explain. It is crucial they understand the hypothesis of both, because their comprehension does seem to moderate and temper their expectations. To me, psychic work pertains to the information I receive from Spirit regarding my client. It is current to the day but it can also predict what may occur in his future.

Dwayne explains he does not focus on a client's past unless to validate the relevancy of another person or event in the client's life. He stresses he does not dwell on a person's past mistakes or experiences, which should be left exactly where they are, in the past. What concerns him is the present and future of his clients, especially if he can help or influence their good choices. "If I merely validate a person's experiences, emotions or thoughts then my function would be limited, but I function as an 'empath' (a derivative of the noun empathy) which means I have the ability to understand someone else's feelings, as though they were my own. I seem to grasp applicable information but neither I, nor anyone else, fully understands the why. It is simply a component of the 'gift.' I admit there are times when my revelations do not make total sense to me or to the client, but eventually they become clear and relevant." Dwayne is confident his accuracy explains why his clients return for additional readings and are incredibly loyal to him.

"To function as a medium," he explains, "is to communicate with the departed, who are on the other side." When one is a psychic medium, he suggests, you can convey or receive messages, however, Dwayne seldom functions as a medium because it makes him feel ill at ease, when he steps out of his comfort zone.

QUESTION 3A

At what age did you discover you had this wonderful but supernatural 'gift?'

Dwayne recollects he was between the ages six and eight when he realized he had the 'gift'. "It became crystal clear almost immediately then because I could envision things around me, others did not see. I realized, even as a young lad, my singular insight was unique and believe me, it was a life-changing revelation."

QUESTION 3B

Did your mother or father know you were so 'gifted,' and if so, did they ever advise you, when you were young, to keep this 'gift' to yourself?

Dwayne becomes pensive and extremely personal as he ponders this question. It is difficult for this writer to dispel emotion when he replies, "I have nothing to do with Rick, my biological father. This fact has left a hole in my soul which only a relationship with him could fill, but this reunification will never happen. His lack of understanding as to who I am has created an irreparable abyss between us, and it is impregnable.

"If I could be certain he would truly accept me as I am or even make an effort, this would be a first step to alter the relationship, but he hasn't and it is likely he will not. During my childhood, he (I cannot call him 'father') treated me as a (expletive) freak and to this day, if he or anyone with whom he associates comes near me, it is extremely upsetting and renders me almost non-functional." Because Readers may be curious regarding his relationship with his father, Dwayne relates a long ago incident that is still hurtful and blocks any further attempt to reconcile. "Some time ago, I flew to the Maritimes where Rick lives and works in policing, to embark on a relationship with him or at least make the attempt to establish an understanding as to who we both are. I wanted to determine if we could coalesce as father and son."

During that time, Dwayne discloses, Rick belittled him, made a mockery of his psychic ability, and challenged him in a most contemptuous way by demanding, "If your psychic powers are authentic, then why not come up with the lottery numbers and walk away with the big prize?" Dwayne tried to explain any use of his 'gift' must be acceptable to the Spirits, and could not be used this way. "Combine this with his attitude as to my sexuality and you can envision why the attempt was disastrous, and why I will never try again."

His rebellion as a youngster was a direct result of his non relationship with his father, Dwayne admits, "But despite every bad memory, there is a part of me who loves him. I think about him from time to time, and admit now and then, I yearn for a renewed relationship. However," he adds, "I also strive to ensure his absence doesn't echo excessively in my life now, as day to day I go about living without him." But now, an elated, more animated, enthusiastic Dwayne emerges in the interview, as he reveals it is his mother, "Who is (expletive) amazing. She knew early in my life I was different, but she always tried to protect me. She ensured I was aware there were curious people who would intrude into our lives, not because they cared about us, but rather because they sought nasty tittle-tattle. These revelations were confounding to me because I didn't see there was anything unusual or exciting to learn about us."

Dwayne sadly admits, "I never listened to her. I was too trusting and obviously my mind set was such that I believed no one would knowingly want to damage or hurt me. I was so stupid!!!!!!. But I always loved people and showed it, and even to this day, I still feel love and concern for others and readily, perhaps foolishly, still exhibit that love. Back then, although this is a recent realization I wanted to be accepted. I wanted folks in our small town to accept that although I was different, I was still okay. I wanted to belong. Is that so wrong?" Dwayne ponders. Even now it hurts and troubles Dwayne because he recognizes his mother definitely endured intolerance within the community back then, and admits this revelation was profoundly slow to come to him. "I now understand what she (expletive) meant when she cautioned me about people, and as a single mother raising three kids, how diligently she tried to keep our lives together, on an even keel. She gave everything to ensure our lives would be calm and conventional, but it is true I received more of her attention, because I was so incredibly unlike my siblings. I was trouble." Dwayne does not believe his mother has always understood or believed in his 'gifts' but when nobody else did, she has always accepted him exactly as he is, and has never tried to change him.

QUESTION 4A

Apart from knowing you had the 'gift' what were you like as a child?

"This is difficult for me to answer," Dwayne confesses, but continues with some effort to explain. "I didn't have a terrible childhood but I hated school. I did not then and still do not easily accept any authority over me. I was and still am extremely sensitive and although I was not a loser, I certainly was an underdog. However, I never, 'ever,' 'ever,' 'ever' could be a part of any circle or clique, I simply didn't fit.

"I realized I was psychic or something (expletive) strange before I turned ten years old, but having to accept I was also gay certainly didn't ensure my already baffling life would become any easier." He remembers wanting to physically damage himself when he was about nine years old, although he couldn't quite explain even to himself why he felt this way. "I just wanted (expletive) to go away." As extremely sad as it is to admit, Dwayne reveals, "I felt so disconnected and although I was a nice kid, I swore a lot, I misbehaved, but my innate sensitivity constantly seemed to compel that I strive to connect with everyone. It was devastating to discover this yearning was something that would never occur and rejection would continue to permeate my life."

QUESTION 4B

Was your childhood ever affected positively or negatively by the 'gift?'

Dwayne refers to the previous question/reply, as he ponders this query. "My childhood was confused, disparate, and anguished," he admits, "and sadly, the compassion and understanding I so desperately needed, was elusive and unavailable." He reflects these negatives had a profound and unfortunately, negative effect on him throughout childhood. "It is difficult to admit," he concludes, "but those old tapes continue to play and replay even today."

QUESTION 4C

Did other children recognize you were different?

"Oh yes, they did," Dwayne concedes, "because I was different. If you asked my mother or one of my siblings, I am sure they would tell you I was a reasonably easy kid to have around, but even I recognized at an early age I was unlike others. Early on, I was fully aware other people felt this way about me and would continue to treat me differently."

The sadness is still detectable, as Dwayne reveals he was intensely sensitive and easily offended by others in school. "I wanted to fit in so badly," he remembers, "but I always also felt so (expletive) odd. I related better and was more comfortable around girls than guys, so you can imagine how this attitude was viewed.

"I remember thinking there was something seriously wrong with me, because I couldn't click with most of the guys, but glancing backwards, I know now it all came down to my sensitivity to others. I didn't want to admit it, but I finally realized the source of uneasiness was solely within me. Because of this, I tried to befriend many different types of people and wanted to believe there was someone in our community who would want to be my friend. It is sad but true to admit, there was no one back then who did." Dwayne recalls when he was in grades eight and nine; he did establish friendships with students, who were ahead of him in school. "I could relate to older kids, perhaps because their advanced maturity made me feel protected. With them, I could unbend and relax, which was something I could not do with kids of my age.

"Growing up in a small town," he admits, "did not offer much diversity because there were few people like me or those who could relate to my deviations. I was gay and I was psychic, and there weren't many residents of our small town who could understand or accept either characteristic. Of course, I too simultaneously tried to understand both of these variables in my character, so it is no wonder others were equally as befuddled as I was."

Dwayne concludes the characteristics he considers to be the most pertinent and important components of his personality did not easily materialize. He admits as a teenager, more often than not, he was suicidal and extremely hard on himself. He recognized he was different but he could not fully comprehend the reason why he was.

QUESTION 4D

What were your teen years like?

"Those years were wild," he admits, "although I did my best in school work, I did not even try to ease the relationship between my teachers and me. I felt they did not like me and perhaps they had good reason."

Dwayne remembers he was coming into his own at the time and although different, he tried cautiously to exhibit the obvious shades of his individuality, by the way he dressed and the music he enjoyed, but he did not, could not, fully or consciously reveal his true sexuality.

"I ALWAYS, ALWAYS, ALWAYS had a huge interest and gravitation to anything spiritual," he admits, and although Dwayne began working when he was 13, he remembers he spent his money to purchase numerous books that explained subjects such as voodoo, shamanism, herbals, séances, demonology, angels, spirits, witchcraft, paganism, and everything else available in the paranormal, as he continued his effort to learn more about these esoteric subjects. "I am self-taught and proud of it," he admits. "I recall it was during these private times when I felt most at ease and even took pride in who I was. Sure I knew back then people found me (expletive) weird, but I tried not to care, and made self-learning and increasing my knowledge mean everything to me. I was finally growing up to accept and like who I was."

Dwayne concludes it was his enjoyment of music which deserves the credit for getting him through his teen years, and even today he finds comfort and clarity of his personality when lost in the music he loves. In the past, he didn't use his psychic 'gift' to find or make friends, but admits he had to learn to accept himself as he was. "I wanted to appear 'normal' to people who were with me day to day.

"Ah, but today is a different story," he reveals. "There are many people who would judge me for being different or might think I am perceptibly reserved or even rude, but I don't think I am. I do, however, listen to my instincts considerably more now because of my lamentable past. I don't rush into friendships. I tend to keep my distance and undoubtedly my unmistakable body language will ensure that others can readily interpret what I am thinking or feeling and respond accordingly. The fears of my teen years are now far away and long ago."

QUESTION 5

How did the revelation that you possessed this 'gift' make itself evident to you?

Dwayne cannot reference an actual time or place in his life when his 'gift' made itself known, but in simple terms he does remember, "I just seemed to know and see things around me when others did not. It was obvious to me, even at a young age; I was exceedingly more sensitive to every facet of life than were others around me. He admits even now he is more finely tuned-in to the esoteric, when he daydreams or is in a calm, placid mood, both of which are critically important to him in his psychic work.

QUESTION 6

What was your first experience in this field?

"I am uncertain if I can actually call this my first time but it certainly involved my knowing there were Spirits or some 'Entities' that encircled me. Talk about a weird feeling," he admits, "because it was like being followed constantly, every day all day long, but I also recognized their misty, steady presence was and still is, a huge and necessary component of my 'gift.' I cannot claim to actually know who my Spirit Guides are, but I do know there is more than one linked to me and despite the invasion, I also feel perfectly protected."

QUESTION 7

Do you envision things before, as, or after they happen, or each of the above? Please give an example of each.

"This is kind of tricky to answer," Dwayne admits. "Mmmmm," he sighs, "I definitely have visions and they generally relate to something presently pertinent or to occur soon." He cites this example. "When I do a reading, a vision can materialize that is extremely strong. It means something will happen soon, but if the vision is foggy or quiet in my thoughts, I then assume this is an event yet to come but down the road. Mmmmm," he signs again, as he says, "I certainly hope this makes sense."

QUESTION 8

Have you ever been incorrect in your readings?

"Yes, I have, but if my clients reject something I might reveal when they are with me, or if something doesn't make sense to them, I am quick to admit it could be my fault for misinterpreting a message or I might misread the symbols that appear to me psychically. I do my best to be specific and detailed in my sessions, but there are no guarantees, and yet, I frequently receive feedback from my clients, who confirm my revelations do come true, more often than not."

QUESTION 9

What, if any, was your worst, most scary or negative experience when using your 'gift?'

"Oh boy," Dwayne exclaims, "this is an easy one to explain. Not getting anything at all from Spirit is dismaying. To be in a session with a client, who is patient but excited, as he anticipates a revelation, but then nothing manifests is upsetting, but it can happen. My psychic ability can go blank, and although my thoughts will journey here or there, they will not focus on the person with me.

"I don't know if I should admit this," Dwayne continues, "but I am nothing if not forthcoming and direct, and there are some people for whom I have done readings, who have passed away. In itself, this isn't too unusual, but the eerie fact is during one specific reading, nothing would come to me and I had no explanation to give to my client. I ended the reading, and it was only later when I mentioned this situation to a psychic colleague, when I realized the client's impeding end of life had blocked my supernatural power to leave me in an inactive psychic state."

QUESTION 10

Do you have a favourite or most memorable client-based session?

"Absolutely!" he exclaims, "and they all involve getting to help kids or young people who are suicidal. To be able to give them hope and faith for the future touches my soul in a way I cannot explain. But when a kid grabs me, hugs me, thanks me and will finally reveal how much I have helped them, my reaction is beyond happy. It is nirvana."

QUESTION 11

How do you acquire your clients?

To reply honestly to this question, Dwayne looks to the past and to the early days in his practice. "My success, insofar as being a respected psychic and medium is solely because clients believe in my ability. In fact, when I first began to read for strangers, it was gratifying and enough for me that at least my mother supported and had faith in me, for offering a service that I couldn't readily and intelligently explain at the time. My boyfriend gave me my first set of business cards as a Christmas gift because he knew, although I was only 18 years of age, there was no going back for me.

To this day Dwayne doubts his friend, "Realizes how dearly I valued and appreciated those business cards because they seemed to affirm who I was, and they were instrumental in my decision to take my 'gift' to the next level, as a 'professional psychic.'

"I mean how many young people have a (expletive) business card at 18? Of course, I could have ordered some of my own but because I looked up to and admired my friend, it was gratifying to know he believed in me. His gift encouraged me to seriously discern who I was and give recognition to those traits that made me who I was. At the time I worked full-time night shift as management in a retail position," which Dwayne describes as a 'dead-end, mind-numbing' experience. "I didn't want to be told what to do and when to do it anymore, so despite limited belief in myself being insecure and scared, it was time to decide my future. But who, I asked myself, will compensate an 18/19 year-old to conduct a psychic reading?

"What is worse to recall," Dwayne admits, "is to remember I also had a DUI (driving under the influence) at the time and I was dealing with two separate assault charges, which were the result of an extremely abusive relationship I had for a year-and-a-half, prior to the one I was then in. It was a frenzied, strenuous time, but even so, I did manage at least two readings every day during the week, all the while I continued to work my shift, from ten p.m. to 7:00 a.m. every day."

Dwayne spent over a year working these 'zombie' shifts, but he constantly worried and wondered how he would ever make something worthwhile of himself and realize his dream to function as a genuine psychic. "I was stressed the DUI could land me in jail. It didn't. Gradually a few calls from people who wanted a reading, materialized. The calls keep coming from referral, my Facebook page, where clients would 'like me' and from the business cards I distributed at every single opportunity."

QUESTION 12

Can you, as a psychic, manipulate the person for whom you are reading?

Hesitation does not impede Dwayne's reply, as he reveals such manipulation solely depends on how gullible a client might be. He gives this example. "If a person is lost in life, obviously unhappy and seeking resolution, she or he may choose to use as a guide the information I disclose, but I firmly believe people also possess freedom of choice and will do what they will.

"However, in a reading, if I predict a love-seeking client will meet a wonderful person, marry, have a family, and live a happy life, I exercise caution before I speak." He explains it is possible a client may use his prediction, perhaps unintentionally, as a blueprint on which to make serious personal decisions, and he or she may forego personal caution and serious thought before becoming involved. "In other words, I can help but I cannot and do not deem as final, information revealed in a reading. Free choice," he repeats, "free choice is predominant in life." Dwayne cautions because his revelations may encourage a client to follow a definitive path, he is exceedingly specific in his readings, will divulge every detail of his psychic revelations to the client, even to disclose the name of person revealed in his vision. "Then it is up to the client to find the person named and decide what happens next." The psychic is adamant his envisioned person will materialize at some time in the client's life, but as to a future relationship, he exerts no influence, therefore, he does not manipulate, he suggests.

"Unfortunately," Dwayne reveals, "there are some people so desperate and unsure of their own identities, they may be tempted to rely too heavily on my readings, so I try to be circumspect and cautious. I am human prone to error and mistakes at 24 years of age, and I cannot claim to have definitive answers to life and its meaning. I want to help people, but my revelations are based on Spiritual disclosures, and my own life experiences to the here and now."

QUESTION 13

Is there ever a time or with a certain kind of person where your 'gift' does not work, and if so, why would this be?

"Oh yes," Dwayne concedes, "especially if I am tired, excited, anxious, ill, or beset by other emotional circumstances at a given time; however, this seldom happens. Psychic work is something I usually find relatively uncomplicated as the power seems to flow into me when needed." But, he admits, "It may be as well, I am simply not supposed to read for someone, especially if a person is desperate or vulnerable, I can find myself at a loss as to what to say and the Spirits, for their own reasons, simply may not guide me.

"Mediumship, however, is quite another matter because one must have a clear and uncluttered mind to employ this paranormal 'gift.' You must be willing to channel for your client to the exclusion of everything else currently happening in your life or around you at the time, and you must constantly function in the session at a prescribed psychic level." Dwayne repeats he does not read for groups or perform telephone readings, because as mentioned previously he has discovered both venues are impersonal. Further, he admits, he has a difficult time placing time limits on a conversation, which is something that is absolutely vital in group readings because of their plurality.

This being said, he tries 'VERY, VERY hard' not to 'feel' too deeply when he is in a large crowd, because he can actually, inadvertently, psychically connect with numerous people who are there. Dwayne admits his psychic powers can collide with his physical being at times, and when this occurs these powers control him, as they flounce from one person to another. "It is mind-boggling," he reveals, "because it is possible there will be several individuals in the group who require my psychic intervention."

QUESTION 14

Do you control your psychic power or does it have authority over you?

This question evokes a surprising reply from Dwayne, "As yet, I don't think I have the best answer for this," he admits, "but this far into my psychic life, it often depends on the day, my mood, surroundings, anxiety, alertness and all the extraneous factions which are part of anyone's life." Dwayne remembers when between the ages of 17 to 21 he began to have the most inexplicable and terrorizing mental episodes one could experience and relates this memory of that time in his life.

"I was in session with a man ---- a rare, perfect, special someone we seldom will meet in a lifetime. I can honestly say he was the only person I ever truly loved, and I am thankful he was with me that day because my life seemed to literally change before me and threatened to disappear in an instant. I couldn't explain why or what was happening but the feeling of being alone was overwhelming. Without him, it would have been unbearable. My friend was there to help me during those attacks when I honestly wanted to die. I do not admit this lightly, and I would not wish such thoughts to burden anyone I know or will ever know in my life." In narrating this tormented time in his life, Dwayne is visibly affected by the memory but continues to discuss the depths of his despair. "It was excruciating, and yet, I also instinctively seemed to know it was only me who could rescue me. I was the only person who could save me from the black hole which consumed my life. I also admit being frightened beyond words as negative feelings emerged, unbidden, unwanted, and yet, so incredibly authentic and desperately debilitating that sadly, even to this day, I must take medication to control the darkness that still filters in and out of my mind."

Although complete understanding still eludes Dwayne regarding his 'gift,' he does recognize anxiety and panic attacks are a 'curse,' although he now believes he has better control over his 'gift' and the attacks. He is absolutely certain these assaults are directly linked to his ability and sensitivity to those around him, whether they are living or dead. When the attacks occur, "I can feel incredibly lonely and isolated, but I work diligently at finding a balance and strive to live life day to day." Health care professionals have confirmed the attacks are authentic, but as far as Dwayne is concerned, his 'gift' is likely the cause, although paradoxically they also protect and allow him to gain complete control over these 'grim forces' when they occur. "My reply then is, 'yes', I do control my ability but the answer is also, 'no,' I do not, because they present numerous, unruly variables. Confusing, isn't it?" he asks, with a twinkle in his eye.

QUESTION 15

Do you consider your psychic power a 'gift' or a 'curse?'

"Ah, finally, an easy question," banters Dwayne, as he exclaims, "Both! I certainly don't know everything and I don't want to. I do believe, however, I can do as I do because the insight is a 'gift' given to me by my Spirit Guides. The information I impart to my clients is my 'gift' to them through my Guides, with the hope it is useful. I want to help, to provide measured insight regarding the various decisions clients must make in their lives, and I so want my insight to be beneficial. Without question my psychic ability is an incredible 'gift' from the Spirit world to me?"

Conversely, Dwayne quickly adds this 'gift' is sometimes a 'curse,' because it can project a dark side. "This is why I constantly remind myself to respect and honour my glorious 'gift,' and further, "I must never abuse or misuse it.

"I don't mind being different from others," Dwayne says, "in fact I have always been considered by others to be peculiar, and in many ways, it is true. I am an outcast but I am also that singular person 'gifted' in the supernatural domain."

Dwayne admits he embraces a deep understanding and empathy for people who suffer severe emotional pain, and he sincerely hopes his paranormal 'gift' will provide a synergetic and comforting experience for every client, in each and every session.

"But helping others can also be a source of pain to my own existence, ergo; caution is necessary. There are times when I am completely erroneous in thinking I am invulnerable and there are occasions when I must constantly remember to protect me. This might sound simple," Dwayne allows, "but there have been instances when I become so engrossed in a reading I will completely simulate myself into the client's situation almost as though I am him. I must be careful to ensure this does not happen."

He admits the paranormal is still a learning curve for him and most vexing at present, is his inability to limit the number of readings he accepts in a day. "There are times when my work schedule leaves me feeling like a 'zombie' and when this occurs, I do not hide this. If I did, it would be unfair to the client and an impediment to my psychic powers, but I haven't learned as yet, to prioritize or say 'no.' I am, however, working on it."

QUESTION 16

Do you have to summon your 'gift' or does it have a will of its own?

"I do not summon it," Dwayne says, "quite simply; I listen for it to arrive. When I am in session, I don't look at the person for whom I am reading, because my complete concentration is centered on listening to my Spirit Guides. Imagine you have ten television sets on simultaneously, but each one at different volumes on various channels, and you will then have some idea as to what occurs for me in a reading, as the Spirit Guides invade my psyche." Despite numerous intrusions from the supernatural, Dwayne concludes he then must make sense of what he is hearing and learning, and then honourably and effectively impart this knowledge to his client.

QUESTION 17

How do strangers react to you when you encounter them? Do they have any idea or realization that you have the 'gift?'

"I get so many different reactions and responses," Dwayne says, "but it can be awkward if I join a group of people, who are just then becoming acquainted with each other, but will also without concern, ask their questions of me. When it is my turn to respond, I admit I laugh and sometimes pause before I reply, but more often than not, I do respond." He doesn't hesitate to discuss his paranormal profession if someone asks, but only if he believes the person is sincerely curious and civil.

Conversely, he acknowledges "if a person is rude, ignorant, or trying to make me appear to be a fool, I am mute. I don't care if I am questioned or if people doubt what I do, because I know my intention is positive and my purpose is to help others. Still, he muses, "I maintain a healthy sense of humour because wit protects me and helps to minimize doubt and ridicule." Dwayne reveals he actually admires and expects skepticism when he meets others. It is healthy for people to question what they do not understand, and to believe without verification can cause unease. But he warns those individuals to be cautious because they just might need his services in the future. "I know I am different but I accept who I am, and it has made me strong psychologically and emotionally. I have learned to protect myself from those who would hurt or belittle me."

QUESTION 18

Once people are aware you are gifted or have psychic powers, do they react with:
Skepticism?
Fear?
Disbelief?

Dwayne admits there are people, after they learn what he does, who have and will react in one way or the other. "I don't go out of my way to tell people," he admits, "because I realize my job is one of the most controversial there is, and I simply don't react well when people question my profession. I am fully aware they may be sincerely and genuinely interested, but there have been those times which will undoubtedly occur again, when the information I share is misused or exploited. So, understandably, it goes without saying I am extremely protective when it comes to my 'gift.' It is sacred to me and I won't allow anyone or anything to denigrate or diminish it."

QUESTION 19

Do your psychic powers ever get you into trouble?

Dwayne's reply is pensive as he travels back in time to say, "Yes, when I was young and learning about myself, and when I had no understanding of my 'gift' or why I was different, I would speak out about my thoughts and experiences because I wanted to trust people and believe they would do me no harm, but it was not the way of my world at that time."

He again mentions how his mother tried to protect him and often advised how extremely important it was to keep certain of his unusual characteristics to himself. "She suggested I share specific details about me with people I knew to be trustworthy, but sadly, I did not listen. It seemed life's lessons for me were to be learned the hard way, and I certainly did discover there is good and the bad, to be found in every person."

Dwayne admits his mother was incredibly prescient, and had he listened, his life would have been less traumatic. "I mentioned earlier I grew up in a very small town, where it was extremely difficult to conceal my 'gift,' but it was also excruciating to concurrently come to terms with my own sexuality. These two parts of me regularly placed me in situations where I felt I was the subject of a witch hunt, belittled and completely misunderstood." "When I was 15 to 17, I began to realize it was vital to protect myself from people who did not understand me or why I was different, which ensured my life was confusing, and at times lonely and onerous. I remember a trusted person who warned me to be mindful of what I did tell others about my life. They will ask," she said. "They are curious, but only a few will truly care about you, while others may misuse your well-intentioned revelations. Sadly, I learned this is undeniably true, for once you reveal information publically it cannot be rescinded and can evoke a negative perspective to my professional life that is difficult to efface."

QUESTION 20

Do doors that would normally be difficult to enter, open for you, because you of your psychic powers?

"Yes, I admit they do," replies Dwayne, "and often I know this occurs for no other reason than because of what I do, but it is also a blessing because I believe meeting new people means new opportunities to grow and develop in my profession." He plans to travel extensively one day and looks forward to the diversity it will bring to his paranormal world.

Dwayne reveals sometimes his clients also become his friends, although not on a regular basis. "I am a social person. I have made some amazing connections with people for whom I have read, and to meet new people generates new opportunities. It is pure pleasure to encounter folks with whom I can develop an instant connection, and when this happens I make a concerted effort to see them again."

QUESTION 21

Are you a healer? What is your definition of a healer?

"As a healer, in specific cases, I can alleviate pain through my ability to connect with my Spirits. It is my voice but it is Spirit's intercession which provides specific remedies to heal, and once this transpires, the client must then react and follow through. As a healer, it is possible through Spirit, to nurture well-being."

QUESTION 22

How do you control your 'gift,' or does it need to be controlled?

In this matter Dwayne is again lacking confidence he is fully in control and discloses he has endured numerous and several absolutely terrifying episodes of uncontrollable fear. He explains this seems to occur when he is occupied in an event surrounded by crowds. "You remember I mentioned my friend who witnessed my intense fear and although he wanted so much to help me, other than moral support he could not, because even I could not explain what was happening to me.

"For example, I remember one occasion when I was about to board an airplane on my way to a needed and fun vacation it happened, and another time it occurred when I was at a live music event. Terror struck without warning. I couldn't smile, laugh or even speak. I felt separated from my body, slurred my words, lost my balance, dropped what I was holding, and began to tremble violently. Control was impossible." Various kinds of lighting can also affect him, and make him feel as though he was falling and completely out of control. "What is worse," Dwayne admits, "I can forget where I am, where I am supposed to be and will have no sense of the present." These admissions, he concedes, can even now portray images and experiences difficult to remember and even worse to verbalize. When this happened, Dwayne states, "I either have to lie down or sit quietly and concentrate on the ground or the floor as I struggle to calm myself. Strange as it is, a drink or a beer does seem to help, in fact, as either one can actually block such episodes."

Dwayne asks himself when this occurs, if he is enduring an astral experience or inadvertently reading a person around him. In other words, he explains, "Am I allowing myself to feel or absorb too much from someone in my presence, because it seems to happen when I unwittingly assimilate with someone near me. Or I wonder if I am having an anxiety attack? I just don't know, but I am working hard to remain grounded and more balanced, when I am out in public. It is difficult to explain or talk about," he admits, "because I have never met anyone who can totally relate to these bizarre circumstances."

QUESTION 23

Is psychic power the same as intuitive power?

Dwayne believes these two 'gifts' originate from the same place. "To me," he says, "intuition is something you research to ensure you enhance your skills as a psychic. Intuition transpires more as a gentle feeling that is difficult to explain. If you have it you will know because there is a difference in what you are feeling, and you are aware of a shift in that cognizance."

He feels a psychic has a heightened intuition, a sensation which is considerably more than just a hunch, a vision or a feeling. It becomes more detailed and enhanced by listening, smelling or experiencing other physical manifestations, which will allow a psychic to actually 'see' when others do not.

QUESTION 24

Can this 'gift' be misused?

"Absolutely," Dwayne exclaims, and then explains because psychics claim to have a divine or spiritual ability which comes from something greater than him; he must nonetheless be and remain in control. He says when he reads for clients, he tries never to express his own thoughts or opinions but rather waits for his Spirits to proffer their message and information. "In order for me to channel, to disclose what I have learned from the Spirits, my greatest task is simply to be there and remain open to the message.

"My primary obligation is to be honest. If an answer to a specific question is not forthcoming, I will say so. Dishonesty in psychics is forbidden." Because he believes religious beliefs, psychic ability and mediumship can be taken to a dark place, it is imperative an honest psychic must counsel a client to never rely solely on or base important life decisions because of a specific reading. "If you use psychic revelations along with your own common sense, this can be a powerful combination." Dwayne admits there are occasions following a reading, when a client may question his revelations or the information revealed which doesn't align with any component in his life. The psychic will admit it could be his fault for misinterpreting a message or misreading the symbols that appear psychically. "I do my best to be specific and detailed but there are no guarantees. Given enough time, however, frequently, I will receive feedback from that same client, who then admits those once inexplicable revelations finally became relevant and meaningful."

QUESTION 25

Is it possible for one with the 'gift' to become arrogant in having it?

"Absolutely," Dwayne admits, "it is imperative a psychic develop the correct balance and respect for this exceptional 'gift.' If we do not, it could well nurture our negative side, and this is something too frightful to contemplate."

QUESTION 26

Do you equate your psychic abilities to your faith and belief in God, and do you believe they coexist one with one another?

"I can't claim to know or provide a total answer to this question," Dwayne responds, "because although I do know where my ability comes from at this point in my life, I don't believe in God or in the devil. These names have too many attributes that for me are quite simply contrived by man."

He expounds his perspective by saying, "Add 'o' to God and you have Good, and take the 'D' away from devil and you have Evil and both are only labels. It seems we are compelled to put designations on things for a variety of reasons, but I find this difficult to do because that 'Someone' (God) is so much more than we are as human beings. To assume one has the ability or the right to judge on behalf of God would be to me, a 'sin' in itself." To further explain his faith, Dwayne asserts if he must label himself and his faith, he would simply say he is spiritual. "Religion is man-made," Dwayne continues, "and we humans are prone to error and flaws. Many sects expound rules that must be followed to attain the ultimate prize, 'everlasting life' when you pass. To me, when one is compelled to live life based on fear of straying from these rules, it limits one from experiencing personal and spiritual growth.

"If people would simply live their lives based on how we treat others and would ourselves like to be treated, this would help to ensure the world would be a much nicer place." To conclude, Dwayne does admit he values the good things he sees in many given religions and admires those people, who find peace and a sense of belonging in their faith.

QUESTION 27

Fanciful as this question is, what is heaven like as envisioned by a psychic?

"Mmmmm, another tough question," Dwayne laughs, and in his youthful, facetious way replies, "I am planning on getting my next tattoo based on this question. It will read, "Fell through heaven and bounced off hell." Humour is certainly a prominent element of his character, but Dwayne becomes noticeably serious when he replies, "I think there is something like a 'spirit world' indeed, there must be because I definitely connect to factors I cannot explain. But to offer proof is something I cannot do because I only know what is true so far for me. The other thing I think about is why there has to be such an extreme degree of separation when it comes to these two places. To me, it is contrived and perpetuated by man.

"This is what I believe. There are higher and lower levels and energies, and because I am only human I don't know specifically if heaven as such does exist. I won't prattle away and claim to share my 'secret knowledge' about heaven in readings or seminars, because I don't know and frankly, I don't think anyone else does either." Dwayne confesses when he contemplates heaven or hell, he equates both as to who we are as earthly individuals. He suggests there are questions we might find prudent and illuminating to ask of ourselves.

1. What are your intentions in life and can you define them?
2. What is your purpose in being here?
3. What is it like for you to awaken every morning and learn you are still just you?
4. What thoughts are with you when you lie down at night to sleep?

"These are just several of the perplexing, interminable thoughts which continually plague me," Dwayne concludes, "but what is absolutely certain for me is the answers remain always to be elusive."

QUESTION 28

How many hours per week do you use your paranormal powers?

"Other than emails and/or calling clients, travel or preparing for readings, I spent at least 30 hours a week with my clients," Dwayne says.

QUESTION 29

Does a psychic believe or know?

Before he replies, Dwayne distinguishes between believe and know. To know is fact that is indisputably true. To believe is based on faith. He continues, "I know I am 'gifted' with the ability to communicate with the other side, and I have a deeper understanding of people which enables me to connect with them on a spiritual level. I believe that Spirit communicates through me. I am a channel, but this does not mean I have the ability to completely explain the difference or uncover the psychic code."

QUESTION 30

Is it true that a psychic because of his intuitive ability and knowledge will have no fear of dying, because of his familiarity with the other side?

"While I don't claim to have answers for those people who want all the details about what happens after their last breath. Certainly no one has ever returned to reveal what does happen after we leave our body, but this lack of information doesn't bother me at this time, likely because I am 24. Still, it seems to me there are some things we will never know, until we experience them for ourselves.

"I am not overly frightened to die," he asserts, "my concern is how it will happen. But it is certain when our time does come; it is certainly a time when we are most alone. I don't want to pass over lamenting I could have changed something and didn't, or regretting why I didn't do a certain something, when I had the opportunity." Dwayne seems much older when he observes, "regret and bitterness can have a profound effect on everyone and although misery does love company, and it seems people, who haven't resolved major issues in life, will be more than likely to pass on alone, regardless of how many people are around. As to an afterlife, I just don't know, but I do know I am in no hurry to find out, one way or the other."

QUESTION 31

Is life for a psychic more tranquil, less stressful, and more meaningful, because of the 'gift?'

This question for Dwayne is emotional. He gives it intensive thought then replies, "I can imagine it can be all of the above, but as I ponder this question and roll it over in my mind, I know there are times when I feel more settled, but conversely, there are other times when I will experience precisely the opposite. Peaceful times come too seldom and I cannot summon at will any reaction because it seems what will be, will be."

Dwayne believes he has 'a very bright side' but if he is profoundly honest, he admits there are at times when shadows will blur his light. "Although I acknowledge there is a dark side of who I am, I try to embrace it, and grapple with the challenge it brings. I am who I am and I am in charge of me or try to be, whether it is sunshine or gloom that surrounds me at the time."

QUESTION 32

Do clients ever become angry or frustrated with the information gleaned from your readings?

"Yes, this has happened on a few occasions," then explains, "if a client arrives for a reading and projects he already knows everything, only to discover what I reveal is not interchangeable, he may then become angry. I don't have all the answers but I definitely connect with what Spirit provides me in a revelation."

QUESTION 33

Who are your clients by way of their backgrounds, professions, etc.?

Bright, youthful, delightful, enthusiastic, passionate Dwayne replies to this question with alacrity. "This is the cool part of what I do. I will read for just about anyone and if a client is pleasant to me, then he is in turn treated exceedingly well. I read for people from every career: lawyers, policemen, medical professionals, teachers, retail workers, psychologists, therapists, musicians, authors, judges, parents who work full time but strive to raise their children in a responsible way and even for retired folks."

Dwayne reveals he has also done readings for sex workers, people, who are members of certain groups with gang or religious affiliations. The list is endless but the point is there are all sorts of people who seek his services and seem to feel comfortable in part, because his sessions are private and extremely personal. One factor is clear to Dwayne. "People do not come to me for my personal opinions and thoughts, they come for psychic revelation and regardless of what I hear or perceive intuitively and I am not judgmental. It is not my role or purpose. I sincerely care for the people I see and take seriously my role in their lives."

Dwayne divulges he spends much of his free time researching artists and musicians with a story that interests him. "I want to know, to understand and further, I seem to be attracted to people who are damaged but who are also survivors. It is imperative in any relationship we get to know the whole person, that we don't simply concentrate on the 'good' and ignore the 'bad' because if we do, then we will not nurture or grow the relationship, I know. I have been there.

"My readings have taught me so much about people," Dwayne concludes. "I see beauty in the scars life can leave on a person and to witness the disappearance of those scars through psychic healing is joyful beyond words."

QUESTION 34

Do you see, or have you seen a spirit, angel, or any such entity in your work?

"Oh yes," Dwayne beams. "I have always heard and felt them around me, but these days they seem to surround me, in a more pronounced way. When I 'read' a person, I will, as a rule, look away from that individual, as previously mentioned. I do this so I can 'listen.' It is comparable to having different people chatting around you while you, in turn, attempt to separate what each is saying." Dwayne admits he doesn't always know whose Spirit voice is coming through, but he believes unequivocally; it will be the client's own Spirit, because those Spirits will often accompany a client to a reading.

QUESTION 35

Given how hard you work in a day, do you have a fear of burning out?

"Oh yes," Dwayne laments. "I am still guilty of not doing my best to take care of me, and finding that balance between work and personal life remains elusive. There are days when I almost forget about me and can become foggy and lose a sense of my own person. When this occurs it is a frightening experience.

"There are other times when I avoid people, even family and friends, and when this happens, I know it is time to slow down and regroup. There are other occasions too, when my persona will actually experience residual aftermath of a reading, which can create confusion and disruption in my psyche. I am learning to take better care of me and prioritize my own health. This is profoundly important because if I do not, there is a risk my work with clients might become inept or confusing."

QUESTION 36

If you foresee illness or death, will you discuss these revelations with a client? If not, what if your 'gift' would encourage a client to seek medical help and may then become well? Or, what if you could change the course of an accident or injury to a person, would this embolden you to speak out?

"I try to pay close attention to what Spirit conveys regarding a client and without arrogance, I am extremely competent at interpreting what I am being shown or told. If I make a mistake now and then or misinterpret a message, I tell the client because it could create confusion in a reading and they deserve to know why."

Dwayne keeps records of each subject and key points revealed to him, and will give his notes to his clients. However, if a client is nearing the end of life "I cannot conduct the reading and end the session. Sadly, this has happened several times but I have and do reveal certain knowledge concerning the impending death of a loved one. I am careful to filter as to how to impart such news, but as to altering certain events, such as accidents or injuries, absolutely, I disclose what I receive. It is what I do." Dwayne concludes his story with these thoughts:

"Being a psychic gives me a deeper understanding of other human beings, on all the various and different levels experienced in this life. Having this profound connection is beautiful and no matter what challenges there might be professionally or personally, it is My life! My obsession! My 'gift!'"

REFERENCES

PSYCHIC DWAYNE SCULLION REFERENCE STEPHEN APPLETON CALGARY, ALBERTA CANADA

Stereotypes exist everywhere in every domain, and in this tenet they are no strangers when it comes to public perception regarding the paranormal and psychics. Many people envisage a certain clientele who may seek these services, however, if you, Dear Reader, harbour any such conceptions, read on, because learning about Stephen Appleton will certainly cause reflection.

His journey in life has been exceedingly different from many others, and although he never had a psychic reading before, Dwayne was highly recommended, so Stephen called the psychic to discuss a private sector business opportunity which perplexed his usual cogent and wise decision-making process. "I was already involved in international business but an opportunity to move domestically had arisen, and I believed further insight which might shed additional light onto the situation, was more than welcome."

A lady friend had given Dwayne a glowing referral, and because Stephen was on, what he terms his own private spiritual journey, which began in April 2013, he was reflective and meditative, due in part to the untimely death of his younger brother. "His passing turned my private life upside down and about this same time, my professional life was also in a state of flux." Stephen called Dwayne for a preliminary talk and as they chatted, the psychic astonished him when he interjected the startling revelation there had a recent death in his family. Stephen was dumbstruck.

"How could he know this?"

Dwayne promptly advised his client to remain quiet and not interrupt because his brother was spiritually present with them, and was already engaged in a conversation with the psychic. Dwayne stunned Stephen when he advised his brother mentioned if he had a question for Stephen, he was to reply with a simple yes or no. His brother then continued by way of this paranormal conversation with Dwayne, to accurately describe the relationship the two brothers had in life. It was astounding, an unbelievable event for Stephen, who was, if nothing else, the most pragmatic of men and almost disbelieving of the actual facts even as they were disclosed to him. "I served 27 years in the Canadian Army where I achieved the rank of Colonel," Stephen states, "and having served in Afghanistan and other middle-eastern countries where numerous experiences unfolded that including meetings with the royal family of Abu Dubai, with whom I shared remarkable events, you can imagine I was completely grounded and decisive. There were numerous other incidents during the time which certainly left me more open-minded about unusual experiences and incidents, ergo; I was more than ready for my experience with Dwayne, atypical as it would be."

Stephen found it remarkable when he was informed face-to-face sessions with the psychic were unnecessary; his readings could occur via the telephone. After the initial call which lasted thirty minutes or more, Stephen was sufficiently astounded with the information Dwayne shared. These feelings remained a part of his psyche for several days and he declares his girlfriend also experienced events predicted by Dwayne in earlier readings. To be perfectly honest, he adds, "We were both extremely doubtful but no more."

Stephen's astonishment continued as Dwayne unveiled three business opportunities available to him, about which he was aware. The psychic then went on to reveal how he should proceed in the negotiations, and then spoke about his daughter. "Every detail was accurate and factual. My parents, who are elderly, were also referenced as the psychic revealed their specific health issues, including his father's colon cancer. You can imagine my relief," Stephen declares, "when he assured me that both my parents would regain their health. Nine months have since passed and I know this to be true."

Despite all the positive and factual revelations from Dwayne, Stephen has had only two meetings with the psychic, because, "It would be dangerous to allow Dwayne's insight to become a crutch or impinge on my own ability to make decisions, either professionally or privately. However, if anything particularly vexing or disturbing should develop or if his clarification would be helpful, I would not hesitate to reunite with Dwayne because there is no doubt, he is my 'go-to' psychic."

PSYCHIC DWAYNE SCULLION REFERENCE SHARRON AUBIN CASTLEGAR, BRITISH COLUMBIA CANADA

Sharron Aubin affirms her reading with Dwayne was 'an awesome experience' although it was also somewhat disturbing when he immediately declared that, "Death seemed to surround me. He was perspiring, his head was drenched, and he didn't know I worked as an aide in a long-term facility where we regularly provide care for the dying," she declares.

Dwayne advised Sharron to have numerous medical tests, including a cat scan and ultrasound, done quickly on her face and upper torso, "But again, what he could not know is I had already scheduled appointments for the following Monday with my doctor. No one knew so how could he, I wondered? It was a profound relief when he assured me everything would be fine and every test would be negative which as it turned out they were."

He also discussed her mother's life to disclose she had three long relationships during her life. "Once again, this was true," Sharron admits, "because she was married twice and in between the marriages, she had one boyfriend for 17 years." Dwayne then referred to another woman who was close to her, but who, because of a fall, was immobile. "Again this was true," she affirms, "this person is my mother's sister, who is afflicted with Alzheimer's and has spent years confined to a wheelchair." Dwayne revealed the number three surrounded her aunt which Sharron confirmed was her birthday, but it astounded her when he mentioned a strong male figure was waiting on the other side for her aunt when she passed. His name was William T. and although Sharron could not confirm this information until later with her aunt, she learned her husband's middle name was Thomas.

Sharron, widowed for more than three years, was visibly moved when Dwayne began to speak of her husband and disclosed he had passed as a result of a chest-area lymphatic condition further complicated by diabetes and Non-Hodgkin's Lymphoma and leukemia. Again, Sharron confirmed this to be true, but, "What overwhelmed me was when Dwayne pointed to the necklace I was wearing and asked its significance. He could not know it contained some of my husband's ashes and meant everything to me."

Dwayne also mentioned the number five and asked if Sharron had miscarried a child. "No, I have four children; however, my husband was the fifth of his mother's five offspring which could be coincidental." He also questioned the significance of 'Blue Stones' in her life, which in reality has two meanings. "The first refers to a candle with a blue stone ring hidden inside which I had recently given to my daughter as a gift, but the second and most meaningful symbol referenced my husband, who before he passed, purchased a necklace and earrings for me set with diamonds and blue sapphires."

When Dwayne revealed my husband was actually laughing at that moment, I responded, "It was likely because the bill for the set arrived after he died and I was left to pay for it." In the reading, Dwayne also asked Sharron if she was getting a tattoo which she was, but when he mentioned she was likely to get another, she again reflected there was no way he could know her tattoo wasn't finished and she had a second appointment upcoming to get it done.

"Suddenly," Sharron declares, "Dwayne was struggling to breathe, similar to one who is suffering the effects of exposure to gas or smoke residues, and it is here Sharron is stunned when he refers to a man who had been close to her in life, and in the vision he had with him a small dog. "My brother-in-law had recently committed suicide by exhaust inhalation and had with him his Pomeranian dog. Talk about an intense revelation," she concludes. "Toward the conclusion of my time with Dwayne, I asked if my recent boyfriend had cheated on me when we were together. Dwayne replied he had not in a physical sense but he did 'see' him spending a great deal of time on the telephone with someone whose name sounded similar to Marilyn. Again, he was right because his daughter was named Carolyn and he did spent long hours with her on the telephone."

Numerous other facts were observed in her reading with Dwayne, Sharron concludes, "but as to their accuracy only time will tell because these events are destined to occur far into the future." Despite the eight-hour drive to consult with Dwayne and although it was but one reading, Sharron states unequivocally, "It was a wonderful experience, my first ever with a psychic, but in every way, it was well worth my time and effort."

PSYCHIC DWAYNE SCULLION REFERENCE KAREN DAVIS NITON JUNCTION, ALBERTA, CANADA

If ever there was an individual who needed guidance whether from a trusted friend or a reliable psychic, it was Karen Davis, because one year before her first encounter with Dwayne Scullion, Karen became a widow at age 35 years, with the added and frightening responsibility of raising by herself, five children age four to eleven. "As you can imagine," she utters, "I was broken and in need of serious counsel to help me define a sense of direction for all our futures."

Karen learned about Dwayne from her cousin's best friend, whose aunt and uncle had met with him in a professional capacity, and were profoundly impressed with his ability. To keep the appointment, Karen had to drive two hours plus, and was accompanied by her stepmother, who asked if she was nervous about the reading to come. "My stepmother was afraid and concerned Dwayne would be a fraud, as were other paranormal readers we had heard about. I examined by my feelings truthfully and felt absolutely peaceful and tremendously excited, because intuitively, I seemed to know Dwayne would change my life and there was no doubt as to how much I needed his counsel." Karen remembers being instantly at ease with Dwayne, because, "He was incredibly sweet, sincere and displayed a sincere interest in my life. When he said I was a beautiful and good person, I felt even stronger and more positive, but he was also extremely blunt during the reading. He was honest, factual and forthright, but he did not buffer his remarks, which assured me his observations were genuine and any advice he would give me would be tremendously helpful."

When the session ended, Karen attempted to shake Dwayne's hand when he responded, "Nope, hon! We need a hug!" For Sharon, who believes people today have lost the personal touch because we are reluctant to be overly friendly and suffer rejection, this gesture was for her, a breath of spring. "Being with Dwayne was like being with family. It was as though we had known each other for years."

Karen recalls when the session started, he initially spoke of her mother and brother, both of whom had passed, but he immediately interrupted himself to exclaim, "You are not really here for a psychic reading but to seek the services of a medium."

"How could he know this," I pondered, "because I made no mention of this? It was eerie," she declares, "or you might call it paranormal but there was no denying it was the truth." Dwayne spoke of her husband's death and revealed details which were unknown to him. "It seemed my husband was in the room with us rendering factual information, and when Dwayne disclosed my husband was incredibly sad because it was I, who found him when he passed away, I was awestruck and silent." By now in the session, Karen admits she was 'over the top' wowed by these revelations; however, there was more to come to leave her even more astounded.

"Dwayne disclosed my husband died of a blockage in his heart and had also suffered a grievous heart attack three months before he passed. When he questioned me as to why, at that moment, my husband was coughing, I had no idea, because his lungs had been healthy and were never a source of concern. Dwayne hesitated until moments later, he said my husband was laughing uproariously, and referred to the coughing. It was then my breath caught in my throat because I realized what my husband had just done for me. He validated his presence. HE WAS THERE! and wanted us to know he was.

Dwayne asked for an explanation as to why every time my husband laughed, he wanted Dwayne to pull his left arm up tight to his chest. By this time, I was so overwhelmed, I could barely respond. "You see, my husband, Cody had the 'dorkiest' laugh, which was so hearty it could induce a coughing fit to the point he might damage his lungs.

"The reading, with its revelations was both happy and sad because it confirmed no matter where my husband was, it seemed he was having a genuinely good time." Karen further explains the arm incident by revealing Cody suffered with cerebral palsy which severely affected his left side. "His left arm was smaller, tight and seldom used, until he started to laugh and then, it would automatically rise up tight to his chest, as he bent over to cough."

When she saw Dwayne replicate this motion it was a beautiful sight, but more of Cody was to come as the reading continued, and Dwayne continued to disclose additional facts and details about his life. "It was as though my husband dominated the reading as Dwayne revealed additional facts and details about him." Karen again emphasizes she was desperately in need of her reading with Dwayne. "I was 35 years old, left to raise five children and completely overwhelmed! I was sad! I was lost! To repeat, I was completely broken! I would get out of bed in the morning only because of my children, and when friends would enquire as to how I was doing, I would automatically reply, 'okay.' But the truth was I too wanted to get sick and die, because somehow this seemed easier than to go on living without my sweet, beautiful husband. Difficult as it is to admit, I didn't even worry about my children because I thought oh well, if I die, somehow, some way, someone will take care of them."

Karen admits her attitude was wrong, perhaps marginally selfish, but she couldn't seem to snap out of it. "It was painful to think of all the events in the lives of our family Cody would miss; he would never see as his children grow up, graduate high school, get married or have families of their own."

Regret and despair seemed to take hold and a path to peace and acceptance of life as it should be remained elusive until she met Dwayne. "After his reading, I experienced a sense of serenity and peace that is difficult to explain, but it seemed a thousand-pound weight was lifted from my shoulders, and once again, the sun began to shine for me and my children.

"In the months to follow friends began to notice and mention how well I looked, and once again I found my smile. I found it after meeting with Dwayne." Karen concludes although she is not a religious person, she did come to realize there is much in life we do not see and cannot understand. But she believes her life is 'here' and her Cody is 'there' watching over his family. "For him and for our glorious family, I will live each day as completely as I can, until we meet again."

DWAYNE SHARES ADDITIONAL THOUGHTS . . .

Before Dwayne completes his story he wants to share additional details as to whom he is as a person, and how he copes with the endless stories of grief, need, sadness and loss, his clients frequently share with him. One does wonder how he grapples with the negativity revealed in reading after reading, when he admits to his tendency to lose himself in a client's story or present situation. "I am vulnerable, which as an advocate isn't good, although empathy and understanding are, but it is a fine line between. I continually remind myself I am a guide, a conduit, whose role is to help a client understand situations and enact resolutions.

"I believe achieving a happy and fulfilling life is a universal goal but they sometimes seem unattainable for many. There are those who strive to find happiness but are constantly circumvented by factors beyond their control. It is for them, I beseech Spirit to help me detect their needs and help their lives become better. As a psychic I have no greater purpose, but it remains imperative to bear in mind whatever might make me content and comfortable, may have no significance for my client. If I do help, I am humbly reminded as to how fortunate I am, to be the recipient of this 'gift.'" Dwayne recalls when he initially began psychic sessions (at age 17) his clients visited him at home, however, because he believes everyone tends to leave something of them behind when gone, he has learned that same residue can, for a psychic, be a negative force.

Home and privacy are extremely important to Dwayne so moving his practice out of home and into an office setting seemed wise. "Home is where I can chill, do nothing with no one around to distract or disturb me." He presently leases a facility in a salon which is working out superbly. "I have one place to call home and my other space, equally sacred, is where I see my clients."

On a personal level, Dwayne admits he lives for music. It is background whether he is driving, showering, on breaks between clients, has company, out for a social evening or getting ready for bed. Music is his strength, his companion and his source of serenity. This admission may seem contradictory because he specifies he actually favours rap, hard rock, and some types of metal music. To many, his preferences would hardly seem to be tranquil.

Dwayne spends much of his free time with friends and certain family members. "I have always had a way of making people laugh and I love the feeling when they respond, but especially if we are new acquaintances." He believes everyone should live in the moment, enjoy the sunshine, socialize and occasionally enjoy a libation to keep the Spirits at bay. "I love to travel and intend to do much more of it in the future. New places and experiences will ensure I continue to grow, to be a better, more rounded and balanced person." Finally, Dwayne's advice is simple: "Slow down. Live your life, and make the most of every minute of every day."

DWAYNE CONCLUDES HIS STORY WITH THESE THOUGHTS

"Being a psychic gives me a deeper understanding of other human beings on all the various and different levels experienced in this life. Having this profound connection is beautiful and no matter what challenges there might be professionally or personally. It is "My life! My obsession! My gift!"

A FINAL NOTE

The interviews are finished. The questions have been asked and answered, and our time together has come to an end, or so I thought it had. But it was obvious Dwayne had more to say, additional thoughts he must reveal so he can be absolutely certain he has correctly portrayed who he is, what he does, and how he does it.

He mentions the use of Tarot Cards in psychic sessions, which he no longer uses, although he does give them considerable credit because their application taught him to trust his intuition. "I do not use them to communicate with the dead," he says, "but I still use them to help me understand people, time frames, events, and other happenings taking place in a client's life."

Dwayne explains he has to look at them all together because the cards have a connection and can define a reading. "If you are psychic or looking for a way to train or strengthen your ability, then I believe Tarot is an excellent way to do this. They can teach you to listen and look for signs from Spirit for pertinent information which helps one make sense of meaning and interpretation. "You learn to develop your own connection to each card, what it means to you but I believe the universe can communicate through me based on what I learn from the cards. If you are going to use a tool for foretelling then it is important to use a tool which could be Tarot Cards or Rune Stones, which illustrate both the positive and the negative side of things. This is life, and it is how I see things.

"Why filter information?" he asks. "Why hide information? If you don't want to relay certain information to a client then perhaps you shouldn't read for them in the first place."

Dwayne admits this is something he is still trying to come to terms with. He doesn't understand why he might encounter an information block, but believes it could be because he is not supposed to know something so Spirit holds back.

"I recently ended 20 different sessions because this occurred. I was receiving nothing and when information doesn't easily flow to me I am uneasy."

However, he adds, he does not meet with a client simply to answer their questions. "If a client wants a reading they must book a session with me. If a person asks questions it is obvious they are seeking specific information about an issue important to them. I then ask if there is anything specific they want to discuss and if so, we do. Other than this example, I discuss only what comes to me and if a client has an important question I will often leave that question to the end of the session." Dwayne opines he is not afraid to say he does not know when nothing comes to him. "I honour this position and trust I am not supposed to know, and hope the lack of forthcoming information isn't because I am not being as perceptive as I usually am.

"I don't think I am supposed to know everything and I do not," he admits. He explains he sees a good or successful TRUE psychic medium, as a person who is wise, worldly and just plain smart. "In my opinion, they know what it is like to endure those darker, more scary times and are not all together certain if the storm will ever end with a silver lining. As mentioned, I don't know everything. I would never claim to and frankly, I never want to."

He asks, "What would be the point in even existing if one knew everything? It would be (expletive) scary. Just think about having the responsibility of knowing the answer to every question articulated by everyone just because they want to know. Some knowledge may be power, but my limitations are self set. I know what I am capable of understanding, but I also know every day is different and special and to be honest," he says, "this is what is most important to me." Dwayne admits when people ask him what he does, he expresses his appreciation because he has been given a psychic 'gift.' Conversely, if a person he meets is ignorant or rude when commenting on his 'gift' morals, motives or his reputation, he will respond accordingly, despite the negative connotation. "I don't claim to have a complete or solid explanation as to why I can do what I do, but I do not back away. I stand my ground. I know what my goal is and it never changes. I want to help people."

Dwayne chuckles when he recalls the number of times a person will berate him for not disclosing the winning lottery numbers and when this occurs, he shoots back with the question, "Do you really think I have an answer for that? Such trivialities are not my function and are beneath the role my Spirit Guide has in my life." Another chuckle emits, when he reflects if he did have those numbers, he would give them out, open a second, exceedingly profitable business and pocket his share of the winnings. "It just 'ain't' going to happen," he laughs.

Dwayne concludes his dissertation by stating if a psychic has prior knowledge regarding a certain topic; he can begin the session feeling more confident and receptive to the reading. "That is the best way I can put it," he concludes, "and that is why I intend to continue to learn and grow both as a person and a psychic for the rest of my life."

For those who have read Dwayne's story and might like to make contact or acquire further information you can reach him:

Telephone number: 403.307.2347
Email: dscull13@gmail.com
Facebook: www.facebook.com/dwayne1324

His fees are determined individually at the end of each session.

Please note that Dwayne has returned to his home town of Sylvan Lake, Alberta.

PSYCHIC

SYD SAEED
LOS ANGELES,
CALIFORNIA
U.S.A.

AUTHOR'S NOTES

Syd Saeed
February 22, 2014
The Book! The Book!

I have been neglecting the book, and although I haven't been writing using my computer, I am constantly writing it in my mind. But something seems wrong, incomplete, something --- a nebulous, inexplicable component is missing. This does not mean I am displeased or unhappy with the topic or the subjects chosen for this work, but the concept has yet to fully materialize. It is deficient and missing a certain ingredient which will bring dimension and depth to the subject. What shall I do?

What I always do . . . head to the internet where I can research, explore for additional background, discover useful, relevant information, or in this case, find the missing link. Every person featured in this work has come to me from referral or my own research, but now I am searching for a special someone I might find online. Which I did.

Meet Syd Saeed.

British born, of East Indian heritage, actor, a managerial background with experience in the music industry, a psychic medium and a spiritual teacher of the Indian heritage, he will undoubtedly have additional qualifications, because it is evident I barely scratched the surface in our initial conversation. It is time to find out if my instincts are correct. Near noon when I send a message to Mr. Saeed, I fully expect any response from him will be slow in coming, if it does comes at all. Still nothing ventured, nothing gained, so it is worth a try.

Click, Message sent.

Barely one hour passes when Syd returns my call and already I know I am speaking to a man who cares deeply about his 'gift,' is committed to his clients of which there are many, is recovering from the first serious illness of his life, pneumonia, which derailed him for several weeks, but on this very this day, is again well enough to escort his wife to a coffee house for their first outing in many weeks. Los Angeles is their home and it is from here Syd plies his trade, is contracted for various movie roles, and enacts at least ten readings per week without charge because, "I am here to serve."

He recognizes there are those people in need but who cannot pay his fee, so his "kind, loving and giving nature' will ensure if psychic insight is necessary, he will provide it." Mr. Saeed, but now a more familiar Syd, as we quickly establish mutual interest and familiarity, volunteers to interpret any perplexing paranormal jargon should I require it, and additionally, he will also advise, correct, or assist me, whether or not he is included in the book. His humble, sincere, admirable comments instantly confirm I have found my missing link.

THE EVOLUTION OF PSYCHIC

SYD SAEED
LOS ANGELES, CALIFORNIA

QUESTION 1

Are you a psychic medium?

"Yes, I am," Syd states, but quickly adds that despite his 'gift' he firmly believes that we, as human beings, are not meant to know everything in advance of our lives. "We are here on earth to grow and learn life's lessons as they present themselves to us, and I am here," he maintains, "to help a client recognize and regard each lesson in serious contemplation."

QUESTION 2

Is there a difference between a psychic and a psychic medium, and will you define each one?

The answers roll off Syd easily, as he explains that psychics gather their information through Spirit Guides, while a medium has a connection to people who have passed to the other side. "Those in the Spirit World continue to have a connection, a channel to impart information from the deceased to loved ones," but he is quick to advise, "not all psychics are mediums but all mediums are psychics." Syd contends this is a well-known fact in the paranormal world and is readily accepted as fact.

QUESTION 3A

At what age did you discover you had this wonderful but supernatural 'gift?'

Syd hesitates slightly, almost as if he is travelling back in time to remember precisely when his 'gift' did manifest, to soon recall he was about five or six years of age. Revelations came to him in dreams and visions, although he had no idea why or what was happening, but he does remember dreams about natural disasters or other events yet to happen but eventually did.

"I would 'hear' conversations my mom and dad might have with each other and eventually did, or I might see a Band-Aid on a child's knee not there earlier, but was the day after my vision. Back then I could envision what would happen on any given day, but as happens when one has a child's perception, I gave this phenomenon little thought. In fact," Syd recalls, "I thought these revelations were normal and all children were similar to me." He remembers as a child, Spirits would appear in his room, especially one with long hair who wore dark clothing. He was not particularly spooky or scary, he was just there, although "I tried to block him out," Syd recalls, "but he remained along with others." He now makes an astounding statement when he equates his early visions to babies who gurgle and coo in their cribs. Syd believes they are actually speaking to Spirits which to him, explains, 'baby chat.' He recalls Spirit Children present in his room when he was a young age, but he was never frightened of them, but rather, accepted their presence as normal and routine.

QUESTION 3B

Did your mother or father know you were so 'gifted', and, if so, did they ever advise you when you were young to keep this 'gift' to yourself?

There is a marked change in his voice when Syd speaks, almost as though sadness lingers which is still hurtful, despite time and his success, as a medium. "My dad passed away when I was 13," Syd conveys, "but because I did not share my revelations with him then, he had no idea of my psychic life. My mom did, but she really didn't want to know."

Syd shares early memories. "My mother arrived in this country at age 16, the mother of two children by the age of 20. As a teacher, she had an excellent command of the English language and was able to find employment." But life was challenging for this family. Over time, his mother finally revealed to Syd that both his grandfather and great grandfather were 'gifted' psychics, but because they lived in a different culture their 'gifts' would manifest in a different way than his did. She said although his ancestors were spiritual, they had little time for organized religion. In 1920s and 1930s India superstition was rife, and the ancestors' 'gifts' were considered incredibly unique and exceedingly exceptional. These same forefathers were frequently called upon to eliminate bad spirits from human bodies, or to cleanse a house of evil beings. Syd never met his grandfather, but was thrilled to learn this special man not only kept a large photograph of him over his bed, but recognized early he possessed the special 'gift.' He would counsel his mother to, "Leave the child alone because Syd is very different." Syd recalls, "It took a long time before my mother finally accepted this fact," and laughingly recalls when he tried to share a psychic event with her, his mother would admonish him to, "Shut up and eat your breakfast."

"It seems she didn't want or couldn't deal with anything paranormal then, but her days were chaotic as the sole support of three children. But finally, she did accept, to become and remains, my most ardent supporter."

QUESTION 4A

Apart from knowing you had the 'gift' what were you like as a child?

"I was shy," Syd says, "and I was chubby but I was good at English and expressed myself well in a group. I was a happy child, who loved football, soccer, baseball, and I lived for Saturdays, when our gang would either play or participate in games wherever we could. I can safely say I was a normal kid in many ways, but what is even more truthful, I wanted to be."

QUESTION 4B

Was your childhood ever affected positively or negatively by 'the gift?'

Syd's response is an immediate, unequivocal "no." Indeed, he maintains his response is likely boring because he remembers giving his 'gift' little attention then. "I probably exerted an unconscious effort to minimize it and from my amazing perch today, it is difficult to accept I didn't know or feel I was different from others, because this 'insight' was omnipresent. Truthfully, I did try to give it little or no thought, but it is likely I did suppress it during my childhood."

QUESTION 4C

Did other children recognize you were different?

"I don't think so," Syd recalls, "but no doubt this was because I concealed my 'visions' and did not speak about them to anyone. Instinctively, I knew they must remain secret to ensure I would not draw attention to my ability to 'see' what others could not."

Syd recalls he worked extremely hard academically and participated in sports, where he exerted prodigious effort to be just like everyone else. "I wanted to be accepted," he admits, "and instinctively knew, even as a child, 'seeing' things would make me indisputably different so I kept anything paranormal to myself." Life changed when Syd turned 13 years old, because it is then, when he literally blocked his 'gift.' It was a turning point in his life, and what follows, explains why.

QUESTION 4D

What were your teen years like?

Syd quickly replies, "They were 'normal' whatever that meant then, until I was 13 in 1982, and my Dad passed away. Losing him changed everything. I rebelled because I recognized my life would never again be the same, and would be so completely different for me. Knowing this made me angry, which in turn, meant that I did all the teen things that screamed rebellion."

Syd admits from the time he turned 13 to age 31, he denounced everything that denoted conformity. "I had my ears pierced when only society's bad boys did this. I smoked, drank alcohol now and then, grew my hair long like Arnold Schwarzengger's and quite literally, went my own way affecting misjudgments and mistakes on my journey. I also began to work in the music business which ultimately turned into an incredibly interesting and successful career."

Syd is emotional when he discusses his mother and the difficult life she endured, partially because of his behaviour, but also because she was a young single support mother, who now had five children to raise. "She was reared in a culture so vastly dissimilar to the one in which we lived, so it took a colossal effort on her part, to adjust to westernized society."

Syd pauses to gathers his thoughts and then continues, "My mom is my hero. If it were possible, I would give her every medal, bestow every honour, right every wrong and in every way I could, credit her for her strength, patience and the love she so readily gives to her children. She is my hero," he avows, "and I admit even today, I carry guilt for the heartache and distress I caused her."

QUESTION 5

How did the revelation that you possessed this 'gift' make itself evident to you?

"After my father died it became more evident than ever before that I was different, and often when I would make certain observations, or categorically express paranormal subjects, kids would laugh at me. They didn't understand, and were heartily amused with my revelations."

This self-effacing psychic now reveals he was a 'fat kid' until age 13, when following his birthday he made a concerted effort to lose weight. He also decided to 'shut up' and make no reference to his 'psychic abilities' and began to block apparitions as they appeared to him. Try as he did, however, Syd could not block his ability to sense psychic forms, or to clearly hear what they were saying to him. To put it plainly, his mind was one busy venue.

QUESTION 6

What was your first experience in this field?

Syd pauses for several seconds, and then recounts a memory of long ago. "I was walking through a shopping centre in England," he remembers, "one of those large facilities who placed someone at the entrance to pass out credit card applications. As the lady tried to press one into my hand, I said I wasn't interested, but we got to chatting and during that impromptu conversation, involuntarily, I uttered the most astounding revelation."

What Syd revealed could well have created an uncomfortable situation when he said in these words, "You are going to get that baby you want soon, but it won't be with your present partner. Rather, you will meet someone new who will be the father of your child." Syd remembers his prediction gave way to disbelief and incredulity which encompassed her face. What was even more astounding occurred when he continued with the suggestion that she must resist getting additional tattoos imprinted on her back because her new partner will not like them." Despite her skepticism this young woman did turn her back to Syd, and slightly lifted her blouse to display a small tattoo on the small of her back, but as to how this man could know such things, obviously confounded and confused her. She also had no way of knowing this was his first reading and it was unsolicited. As he walked away, Syd was equally deeply affected as he questioned himself, as to why he felt compelled to speak to her as he did.

"It was obvious my remarks left her befuddled. Why would I, a total stranger, make such predictions regarding her personal life, her wish for a child and without hesitation, also predict a new liaison with another man? It was simply beyond the pale," Syd admits. "About six months later, almost as if another meeting with this young lady was preordained, we met again, but this time not in the store, but rather, on the street. I felt a faint tap on my shoulder and looked down to see a lady; barely 5'1"(I am over six feet) determined to get my attention."

Syd had forgotten the earlier encounter, until this lady, displaying a radiant smile, pointed to her stomach and exclaimed she was expecting a baby with her new partner; he was then reminded of his earlier predictions. Her disclosures validated his foretelling and despite their rather bizarre meeting in a large department store, his first psychic revelation was proven true. Even today, much further down the road, this memory for Syd lingers clearly and vividly.

QUESTION 7

Do you envision things before, as, or after they happen, or all of the above? If you can give an example(s) of each it would be beneficial?

Without hesitation Syd responds, "Absolutely before" and mentions his dreams which will continually emit messages from beyond to him, but perhaps even more astounding are visions which appear daily in his psyche. "I receive warnings something is about to happen to a friend or a client, and the urge to call that individual with advice to do or not do something, is incredibly intense."

Syd explains his 'vision' might depict something as niggling as to whether he advise someone not to sell a house, but rather wait a few days before making a decision. Then there also are occasions when the revelations are serious and demand immediate action. He recalls such an event when a young couple arrived at his home for a reading, and Syd, without hesitation, was able to reveal an urgent event which required their immediate attention. The man mocked his 'vision' but the lady took his disclosure seriously and planned to take his advice. Syd takes such negative reactions in stride because he believes a competent psychic often envisions many things, some of which can be altered and some of which cannot. Most of the time his clients validate his predictions, even to exclaim during a reading, "Oh, that makes perfect sense," and more often than not, Syd is proven correct in his readings. "I don't wish to appear arrogant, however, over many years, I have developed a reputation as a psychic, who has excellent timing and accuracy in readings, which is encouraging, as I continue my work. I am incredibly blessed to do what I do."

Syd firmly believes in past lives and he surprises me when he exclaims he and I have known each other previously during past lives. I question why he feels this way, and he responds simply and quickly. "Because we blended so quickly and effortlessly." He concludes many people will proclaim upon meeting him for the first time, they are certain they have known him for a long time, but "it is seldom the feeling is mutual." Again, he surprises me when he declares, despite our fledgling relationship, we did know each another previously and explains, "Life is all about energy. It is fact that a person's individual energy will immediately recognize a relationship from the past. Once confirmed, there is a gentle ease into conversational intimacy." Perhaps this is also helps to explain an 'aura' which many people will experience upon meeting another for the first time.

QUESTION 8

Have you ever been incorrect in your readings?

Without hesitation, Syd replies, "Absolutely yes! But I am seldom wrong in my revelations or predictions. I can be out on the timing of an event or occurrence, because I filter information as a conduit and I am human. I make mistakes." He hastens to add, "It is not my ego speaking now but seldom if ever, do my clients allege I am mistaken or I have miscalculated an event.

"Clients don't seem to mind if I make a mistake regarding timing in a reading, as long as the prediction occurs. We, as human beings, have free will, which means the timing of a prediction can alter back or forth and miscalculations can occur. I also firmly believe there are some issues which cannot be altered or delayed. Events have their own agenda, so all I can do is convey the information received from my Spirit Guide. Beyond this," Syd concludes, "any action taken as a result of my prediction is solely up to the client."

QUESTION 9

What, if any, was your worst, most scary or negative experience when using your 'gift?'

Syd reveals he will infrequently encounter a negative situation because he emanates from a 'place of good.' "Before my sessions," he reveals, "I meditate and commune with my virtuous Spirit Guides, who will at times create situations whereby I am to be taught a lesson, say for example, in humility. But there are also times when my Spirit Guides will notify me if I leave a channel open. This is for me a warning that gets my immediate and serious attention, otherwise, I leave myself open to grievous negative risk." Grateful this situation does not occur too often, Syd unequivocally believes it is only because he is blessed and protected by his Spirit Guides.

"Despite the protection, however, there are some things I will not mess with. For example, Ghost Spirits for whom I have intense respect. Twice in my life I have encountered Ghosts which were even to me, as a medium, frightening and chilling." He remembers the hair on his head stood straight up and his relief was palatable when they disappeared without incident. He will have nothing whatever to do with the Ouija Board and believes innocent people, who in their quest for paranormal fun use this device, should be cautious, because they could encounter malignant Spirits. Syd concludes he avoids negative situations whenever possible and counts on his Spirit Guides to protect him. "I am a humble person with an extraordinary 'gift' but truly, I am nothing without God and my Spirit Guides. As to why I have this 'gift' I do not fully understand. But what I do know is my genuine objective in life is simply to help people and it is this objective which explains, at least partially for me, why I have been blessed with his psychic 'gift.'"

QUESTION 10

Do you have a favourite or most memorable client-based session?

"I do," Syd responds, "but it requires a backwards glance because it marks the first time I communicated with Spirit, and it DID materialize in a most unusual way."

Long ago and early in his psychic life as stated, Syd frequently did pro bono readings for people who needed his insight but could not afford to pay him. So it was during this well-remembered initial Spirit session when he was in the company of a Hispanic lady, who worked in a nearby coffee shop, and with whom he had briefly chatted in the past.

"Ours was a superficial relationship," he remembers, "but in those early conversations, I quickly realized she was someone who needed help. It seemed she would be receptive and listen to me, if I made the effort in what was for her, a serious and sad situation."

Syd learned this forlorn lady had given birth to twin sons when she was young, but tragically, one of her babies died at six months old and only recently, the remaining twin passed away at age 26. Her grief was palatable, as was her urgent need for help, so Syd called on his Spirit Guide for assistance. What occurs next is uncanny because a Spirit, called Jonathon, emerged. I didn't know the name of her son, who had recently passed, but asked her, 'who is Jonathon'?" Momentary silence resulted as she absorbed my question, and then exclaimed, "He is my son."

"He is here with us," I revealed, "and it was then Jonathon began to reveal incidents to his mother only she and he could know. He spoke of events, personal family history, and disclosed to his mother the last words she had spoken to him, as she sat beside him in the hospital and only minutes before the virulent strain of pneumonia, finally terminated his struggle."

It was the most astounding, incredulous encounter Syd can remember, as Spirit summoned Jonathon, who, for a full fifteen minutes, provided comfort and solace to his mother. Syd, whose voice conveys the joy he too felt from that session of so long ago, has no doubt this woman who had suffered the loss of two children, found solace, comfort and freedom from her excruciating pain of loss and despair.

Earlier, in their fledgling relationship, this lady had cared enough for Syd to encourage him to use his 'gift' as a business and accept fees for any assistance he provided. He believes in conjuring her son during that psychic session, was in a small way, repayment to her, for having confidence in him.

"She was instrumental in my decision as a fledgling psychic to take a chance and develop what is now a busy and successful business." Syd believes his Spirit Guide, as a boon to him, revealed those pertinent events through him and Jonathan, to his mother and in doing this, set him upon the path he daily traverses to pursue his preordained calling.

QUESTION 11

How do you acquire your clients?

Syd advertises his services on only one website called, The Best Psychic Directory, but contends the majority of his clients come from referrals and recommendations from past or present clients. "Word of mouth from happy clients is by far the manner in which clients come to me and just as people can experience difficulty in locating a good mechanic, so can they experience decisive issues when they want to connect with a reputable psychic.

"I always try, especially with new clients, to make them feel comfortable and although they may not always be pleased with my revelations, because the results they seek are not always immediate, I do try to ensure their experience is as congenial and specific as possible.

"But yes," he reflects, "it is almost always clients come to me by way of referral from satisfied, and for the most part, pleased clients."

QUESTION 12

Can you, as a psychic, manipulate a person for whom you are doing a reading?

Although Syd hesitates, his reply is "yes" followed by an immediate "no" and instantly offers this explanation because it seems this is an obvious contradiction. "There are people who do not believe in psychic phenomenon and will react to a reading with rude behaviour and often a bad attitude. However, despite the negative attitude when this happens, I still proceed.

"I will not, however, cajole a person into participating in a session because if they are not committed, then neither am I." Syd admits now and then such a meeting will occur despite his resolve, but once he aware this is happening he ends the session. "A client must believe in my psychic 'gift,' and further, that I am genuine or the reading will fail." Despite obvious reservations, occasionally Syd will relent to do a reading for a skeptic, only to witness the abrupt alteration in the attitude of the non-believer.

There are also times when a doubter will return to Syd to regretfully reveal although the revelation at the time was not to his liking, he should have paid attention and been wise enough to nullify what was predicted would be a negative situation. 'Too late, too late,' is a common refrain with them. Syd concludes, he will seldom as time goes by, visually recognize a person who may have expressed doubt or disbelief during a reading, but declares a client will frequently remember him, his accurate predictions, and as stated, will say so. "In this there is sweet satisfaction," he declares "but not because I want to be right, but rather because their disclosure shows respect for my profession."

QUESTION 13

Is there ever a time or with a certain kind of person where your 'gift' does not work, and if so, why?

"It can happen," Syd admits, "but seldom does, although there are times when I receive information that I am not meant to pass on." He recalls occasions when his Spirit will decide if he should reveal certain information to an individual client, but states there are also times when his Spirit will counsel that a certain client is not yet ready to receive a message, until after a particular life lesson has been learned.

It is a rare for Syd to be prohibited from hearing or intercepting a message from his Spirit Guide, or when, during a reading, the flow of energy between them is blocked, no message is received, and he is offered no explanation as to why. But he has also learned there is nothing he can do to alter or force communication when these barriers occur.

Syd reveals there are occasions when his Spirit Guide will automatically protect him from people who might abuse or misuse him, and concedes that all psychics, every now and then, will encounter those people who do not believe, are openly critical, and may even call the psychic a liar or unethical. The moment Syd encounters such a situation he immediately ends the session, and if payment for services had been made, the fee is returned. "Why would I take money from such a person?" he asks. "My relationship with a client is no different from any other, in a given community, whether it is a psychiatrist, who counsels his patient, a mechanic, entrusted to ensure an automobile is safe and secure to drive, or a grocer, who markets safe products to his customers. Each one of us must have the consumer's trust, and in my case, I cannot interpret if confidence in me is missing."

Syd concludes he has encountered clients who feel his psychic insights are a special 'gift' but he is wrong to charge for his services. He contends, however, that money is a necessary evil, can be a powerful asset, is a tool with which to bargain, and is essential to sustain life." However, as he stated, if Syd perceives a potential client cannot pay, he does not charge, and trusts in this small way, he is using his gift, wisely and generously.

QUESTION 14

Do you control your psychic power or does it have authority over you?

Syd responds promptly. "Most of the time after I tune in my psychic energy I am in control, but there are times when I can become disconnected with my Spirit Guides, although this does not occur too often."

In fact, he asserts, generally the opposite is true because frequently the information that comes from the Spirits, will flood his mind unbidden and in an unearthly way. "For instance," he relates, "I can be walking in a store, pass a person who I have never met or seen before and yet psychically recognize a loved one of this individual has recently passed away. My compulsion to impart a message from the other side is so incredibly intense, I have to force myself to walk on by and say nothing.

"You learn to shut out certain revelations, especially in such situations, but doing this is extremely difficult," Syd admits. "Additionally," he advises "a psychic must be constantly be aware there are those dishonourable Spirits who also present themselves to me, but whose intentions are negative and nefarious. Once they acknowledge you are a bona fide psychic with the ability to channel, they can bombard your psychic with information to involuntarily pass along." Syd admits these revelations can occur when he least wants them to, but he will then engage his protective shield, and in doing this urges them to disappear and leave him be. If they do not, he simply ignores their presence and expunges their information.

QUESTION 15

Do you consider your psychic power a 'gift' or a 'curse?'

"A 'gift' always! Never a 'curse' even when Spirits barrage me with information, it is still a wonderful 'gift.' "Syd adds there are others who possess paranormal powers but remain non-working psychics, sometimes because they have been disappointed in, or will misread a revelation. He attests when one fully connects with Spirit, who render psychic knowledge in the first place, there is a sense of certainty the prediction will occur, although it can take time.

"Patience is essential," he counsels.

"Perhaps I am incorrect but to me psychic ability can manifest in two ways, one in the knowing and the other, in the actual happening. Some seers are impatient and become despondent if their predictions do not manifest immediately."

He readily confesses it is seldom, if at all, when a psychic can foretell his own future. "It does not work because our emotions cloud our visions which is why a psychic, who wants or has personal need for a rational reading, will seek a trusted colleague to intervene for him."

QUESTION 16

Do you have to summon your 'gift' or does it have a will of its own?

"It is six of one and a half dozen of the other," Syd laughs, "my Guide is there when I want information, but he can also inundate me with data when I am off guard. Yes, it is both," he muses, "but to quantify, I would say seventy five per cent of the time I am the one to instigate a connection to Spirit, but the remaining time Spirit will swamp me with revelations, whether I want them or not."

QUESTION 17

How do strangers react to you when you encounter them? Do they have any idea or realization that you have the 'gift?'

"No, most people do not know and to be candid, there has never been a single person, when we meet socially or otherwise, to determine I am a psychic. The exception," Syd adds, "is when I meet another who is highly spiritual; because it is true psychics will often and unintentionally seek out like-minded colleagues in a crowd, and once found, forge an immediate connection."

Syd reveals these encounters can occur in a store, a parking lot, at parties, or absolutely anywhere at all, and submits even younger people will approach him to chat without knowing why they do. "Folks tell me I emit a definable spiritual aura which seems to encourage contact, but I completely accept psychics are kindred spirits which ensures when we do meet one another, our personalities instantly relate."

QUESTION 18

Once people are aware you are 'gifted' or have psychic powers, do they react with?

Skepticism?

Fear?

Disbelief?

"Effectively, I experience every one of these reactions," Syd asserts, "but it is the encounters with non-believers that prove to be the most interesting. They do not hesitate to express their skepticism, nor do other people who are concerned with what I do, and may feel they are at risk." It is interesting to Syd when a person will hastily declare, 'I don't want to know anything,' although he attributes this more to ignorance than actual fear.

"I never propose a reading to anyone and I never will," Syd declares, "because this would be an unacceptable invasion of privacy. However, when information regarding a person in my presence does manifest in what is for me then, a non-working setting, truthfully, I will reveal my psychic ability, and then divulge I may have pertinent personal information for them. Generally, they want to know more despite their incredulity, but later they will also express gratitude for the heads-up on what they learned." Syd never doubts his accuracy in a reading because he firmly believes it comes from Spirit. To him, Spirit is never wrong, but for people who disbelieve, who are wide-eyed and skeptical when it comes to psychic insight, he will make no concerted effort to convince them otherwise. Syd admits there are times when his gentle words will erase doubt and to substantiate his conviction relates the following anecdote.

It involved a friend of his who wanted to convince his colleague, a non-believer, the gift Syd has is authentic. "Please," my friend requested, "tell me something, anything, I can reference to prove you are a tried and true psychic." He also asked Syd to reveal something personal which his friend would quickly recognize related specifically to him. Ultimately, it must also be current so as to efface any doubt of prior knowledge.

'Spirit Guide' was rather amused by the request, and said, "Tell the doubter he will wear a pink shirt to the interview he is going to tomorrow." Believe it or not the guy admitted he had just selected shirt he would wear, and yes, the shirt was pink. The friend was thrilled when he exclaimed, "See! I told you he was genuine." His pal replied, "Dude, I believe you because there is no way anyone could know I selected the pink shirt, and despite my earlier skepticism, facts are facts." This tale might seem to be a tad frivolous, but Syd and his Spirit were at least able to convert the disbeliever all because of a pink shirt.

QUESTION 19

Do your psychic powers ever get you into trouble?

"I would say no," declares Syd, then laughs as he admits his revelation to a worried spouse regarding an extracurricular affair could be the source of serious trouble to the cheating partner, but disclosing such information doesn't bother Syd at all, because he remains neutral.

QUESTION 20

Do doors that would normally be difficult to enter, open for you because of your psychic powers?

"Definitely! Yes, they invariably do," concedes Syd, but quickly adds, he is reclusive and as such is apt to stay aloof and selectively alone as much as possible. "I see myself analogous to a foreman on the job who must be helpful but distant. My dominant function is to help others and this will regularly override my need to be solitary and separate from others." He admits, however, he endeavours to keep himself at an emotional distance from other people as much as he can, because in doing this he is assured his pathway will remain uncluttered and well-defined.

Syd maintains there are psychics and then there are psychics, some of whom are hailed as champions in the esoteric paranormal community, but their prestige is verified only if they are true to their profession. He firmly believes paranormal ability is a 'gift' given by the Grace of God and does not emanate from within the psychic. Because of this, Syd can feel detached and solitary in some ways, but being alone is no problem because he is equally convinced, his sole purpose is to use his psychic 'gift' to serve others.

QUESTION 21

Are you a healer and what is your definition of a healer?

Syd hesitates before he replies, "Although I may possess healing capabilities, I also consider the category of healing and healers to be a 'most dubious subject.' I don't want to label myself in this way," he submits, "but then again they are people who trust my readings to be truthful, accurate and factual, and who claim my revelations do heal in certain situations."

However, Syd maintains the definition of 'healer' in the paranormal sense is overrated. He recognizes the name is used by other paranormal professionals, including Reiki masters, who occupy a realm he will not enter. Syd claims he is a simple, down-to-earth, traditional psychic and as such, is one who is firmly anchored in his predestined calling, and doesn't want or need to become a healer. "This," he admits, "is a personal bias and not a criticism of those in the practice."

QUESTION 22

How do you control your 'gift' or does it need to be controlled?

"I can control it," Syd states, and then likens his ability to a light switch he can turn on and off. Then he admits, "There are times when the similarity is more akin to a fuse box where events command themselves.

"I am extremely careful to ensure the information I receive originates from my Spirit Guide, or another Spirit with whom I have a connection. Before a reading I seek protection for myself and admit there are times when I am instructed to 'hold back' because the timing to reveal a message is wrong. I am told to close the portal, and I always respect the counsel given to me by Spirit because it is the only protection I have in the paranormal domain."

QUESTION 23

Is psychic power the same as intuitive power?

Syd believes they are definitely different, because "psychic energy is a unique and exclusive 'gift' granted to only a select few." He admits he cannot explain why certain individuals are recipients of the 'gift' when others are not and opines, although some individuals may be intuitive, it is impossible for them to read or predict future incidents for others. "Further," he declares, "they do not develop their innate ability because simply put, they may be unaware they have it."

QUESTION 24

Can the 'gift' be misused?

"Emphatically, yes," exclaims Syd, "because there are sharks out there that will harass and take advantage of vulnerable people by projecting incorrect information in a reading, or they will impart fear in a client by predicting illness or death.

"Never, ever, are psychics supposed to cross these lines," he declares, "and when this happens, I am disgusted." Syd remembers a most unpleasant experience of years ago, when he was himself the client of a psychic, who misused his abilities, and then created havoc in his life. Since then Syd has learned to protect himself in paranormal circumstances, even as he strives to remain open and receptive to his clients.

Syd abhors psychic charlatans who abuse and misuse their clients, overcharge, and render quantity not quality, because they perform too many readings during their working day. "How many readings can one do in a day?" he asks, but then states he does not fault colleagues who have achieved wide public recognition, and can subsequently charge more for their services. He reiterates although his rates are on the higher end in his profession, he still does gratis readings for those who cannot pay. "Believe it or not because of this, I generate criticism from my fellow psychics, who question my motivation."

QUESTION 25

Is it possible for one with the 'gift' to become arrogant in having it?

"Yes! Absolutely! One must be extremely careful to remain humble and work for the greater good, to serve and not be served," Syd emphasizes, "but this does not mean a psychic should be denied from earning a viable living. Our profession," he opines, "is dissimilar to that of a doctor or lawyer because there are no set standards, no qualifications and no regulations which serve as a psychic template. This means anyone can create a website and claim to be a psychic, although such people will be shunned by the legitimate professionals." Syd admits this is the reason why he strives to stay close to himself and work alone, so he can help and not hinder his clients. "It is all about control," he concludes.

QUESTION 26

Because you believe your 'gift' came from God, can it be purloined by the devil or evil forces?

"If I open an unsafe portal it can," concedes Syd. "I have seen this happen when psychics cross over to the dark side because they have become involved in the underside of psychic life, stray from the light, and ignore the pure forces of healing."

He explains there are times when those with the 'gift' unwittingly open portals by being dishonest and unethical and forget why they have been 'gifted' with paranormal abilities in the first place. "We are here to help people and as do other professionals, we must grow and continue to learn every day. We are vulnerable and open to negativity, and to my way of thinking, it seems the more successful we are, the more we are open to temptation and dangerous influence, by those with ulterior motives."

QUESTION 27

Fanciful as this question is, what is heaven like as envisioned by a psychic?

"If one believes in heaven and I am not saying it doesn't exist as such, then believers and the good living will ascend to that place. It is then they will be asked what denotes perfection for them, which will become their reward. In others words," Syd explains, "that which will ensure they are eternally blessed will happen, but I do not call this venue heaven. To me, it is crossing over to the other side, although I do not denigrate those people, who prefer the description, heaven."

To Syd, when one does cross over, the experience will comprise the various stages of healing and growth. There will be those departed spirits, who are sent back as revised persons, and must relive a life where they are destined to learn and mature, while departed others will attain a more elevated status. But for all, he has been told, the learning continues forever, and although "I don't use the term heaven," he says, "I know a celestial home exists for all of us."

QUESTION 28

How many hours per week do you use your paranormal powers?

Syd estimates he is in session from 30 to 40 hours a week with clients, but this does not include the email or telephone calls he receives from other clients during the day. "I do an average of two readings a day but often, I will do more, and although it is demanding and exhausting, I wouldn't change my calling or my work day for any other. I love what I do, and despite having tried other interesting careers, this is my world, tried and true."

QUESTION 29

Does a psychic believe or know?

"It is both," Syd claims, "I know because I believe and conversely, I believe because I know." He has no doubt because it is Spirit, who renders all information." Syd maintains he has a sweet intimacy with his Spirit and utterly believes the information given to him is factual and true, because as he says again, "Spirit is never wrong."

QUESTION 30

Is it true that a psychic, because of his intuitive abilities and knowledge, will have no fear of dying because of his familiarity regarding the other side?

"It depends on the individual," Syd contends, "because psychics are just like anyone else, and are human beings first and psychics second." Although he firmly believes in a heavenly paradise, Syd chuckles that he is in no hurry to cross over, until it is his prescribed time to do so.

"As psychics" Syd reveals, "we channel words and information, although it can be difficult to hone in on the age one might be when they pass, but in a way death might be easier for me, because I know all about the afterlife. Believe me, 'heaven' is a wondrous place," he contends, but quickly adds that "life on earth is tremendously good too, so I am in no hurry to make it to my celestial home.

"I honestly do not fear death or passing on when my time comes, but I have much to do here before I leave." Syd concludes everything in life has a time to live and a time to die, and he is grateful because he knows unlike many people in their lives, he will make the most of every hour of every day before his life ebbs.

QUESTION 31

Is life for a psychic more tranquil, less stressful, and more meaningful because of the gift?

"Absolutely yes! Syd exclaims, "but I am certain my 'gift' is not solely responsible. Learning to be calm, to think outside the ordinary human non psychic box, to develop my own innate, and earnest beliefs and attributes, have combined over the years to make me the person I am."

To further explain, Syd recounts how his personal growth enabled him to give up alcohol at age 42, which was a habit he had acquired later in life at age 35. "Three years, five months ago, I underwent an epiphany and decided I would never again use a mood-altering substance and I never have. I finally recognized alcohol was interfering with my psychic ability.

"Imagine this," he continues. "I have a morning reading scheduled with a client while alcohol remains in my system. For me, there is no doubt it would block my ability to receive information, and most assuredly, it is a deterrent as to how I would communicate both with Spirit and my clients. Alcohol and the paranormal are adversaries," Syd declares, "although I do not advocate abstinence for my psychic colleagues, because I believe to each his own."

QUESTION 32

Do clients ever become angry or frustrated with the information gleaned from your readings?

"I am extremely blessed in this," Syd asserts, "because this has not happened to me. My clients are incredibly respectful although there can be frustration with my insight. For example, a client's heart may desperately want to hear the exact opposite of what is revealed or they may be told something they don't want to hear. This is certainly a letdown but I have never encountered anger or abuse, although I have certainly witnessed disappointment."

He remembers situations when a client was set on being told something specific, for example, that a certain love interest will become a desired partner. "And then I reveal this particular relationship won't materialize. Several clients will become subdued, reflective, disappointed and even leave before the reading is over." But it is also true many clients return later to inform Syd how happy they are with their new partner. "It is gratifying but not surprising," he concludes, "because I can only reveal what I am told."

QUESTION 33

Who are your clients by way of their background, professions, etc.?

"They come from every walk of life," Syd affirms. "I literally read for people from every continent there is. I have clients who are doctors, lawyers, housewives, teachers, therapists, psychiatrists, and although initially, they may exhibit skepticism, I am still approached because we all have issues to probe.

"The questions," Syd declares, "can be as routine as 'will I get the job I want?' or 'will I meet that special someone?' to the more complex issues of health or financial security. I can only respond as the information is revealed to me," he affirms, "but once I do the information cannot be altered or amended."

QUESTION 34

Do you see, or have you ever seen a spirit, angel, or any such entity in your work?

"It was an angel who initially urged me to become involved in the world of the paranormal," Syd relates, and discloses this event is a happening he will never forget. "I was 31, working in the music business where I enjoyed achievement and success to the point I had no intention to switch careers, until that is when I was visited by an angel.

"It was three a.m. and although I woke up, I thought I might be dreaming when an apparition appeared in my room. Talk about hard to believe your own eyes but I clearly remember hearing a voice that manifested in the room as a bright light, but with no visible head. But the voice, out of nowhere, spoke to me for about 20 seconds to say:

'You are meant to be known, to help people, to reach out and open a spiritual path for others. To do this, you must be sober and clean-living,' and then she was gone." For Syd, the angel's message triggered a life-changing moment and although he does not precisely remember every one of her words, he immediately began to alter his life. It was an onerous challenge, but one he was compelled to take, and one which in time, proved to be exceedingly rewarding, because now he daily lives his destiny.

QUESTION 35

Given how hard you work in a day, do you have a fear of burning out?

"I think more about the fear of burning out than actually burning out, but I do pace myself. I do not work seven days a week and I take two days a week to recharge." When Syd is at work, he claims he is extremely careful with his time and explains why. "I do not like those long waiting times some psychics seem to have before an appointment can be confirmed. I have been told there are psychics, when requested by potential clients to arrange a session, advised the client there is a long waiting list before they can be seen, which I feel is unnecessary and is certainly not my style."

Syd is careful not to criticize other psychics, and recognizes although you cannot please everyone all the time, burnout is possible. His caution is worthwhile, he declares, because clients regularly return to him for their psychic needs. "I earn the money I am paid," he avows, "because I maintain a steadfast energy level, and I strive to ensure every reading is honest and sincere." If Syd is not well he will not read, because his good reputation is everything to him and further he declares, it is critical every client at every reading receives only his best effort.

QUESTION 36

If you foresee illness or death, will you discuss these revelations with a client? If not, what if your disclosure would encourage a client to seek medical help and may then become well? Or, what if you could change the course of an accident or injury to a person, would this embolden you to speak out?

"About death, never!" exclaims Syd, who adds, "I am not God, and it is not my place to convey information which is His realm alone. If Spirit did impart such a message, I would never divulge it or speak of it to anyone."

But when it comes to illness, Syd admits although he treads carefully, illness is a subject he will discuss, and recounts a recent reading with a client who was embroiled in a difficult relationship with her mother. Although fully aware of the situation, he was also cautious and circumspect when he asked if the client would mind a question from him. This is unusual, Syd says, because he will seldom if ever question a client, but felt it was necessary in this reading. "Is there someone in your life who has cancer?" he queried, because this was the information his Spirit had previously conveyed. Syd contends once the issue was in the open, his paranormal ability to render advice enabled him to suggest a gentler path this young lady could follow with her mother. Doing this did improve the relationship, he remembers, which was something he sensed needed doing, especially given the grave circumstances of the mother's health.

Syd concludes although he will carefully broach a situation involving illness, accidents or injuries with a client, he is extremely cautious both in his approach and in his revelation. "My purpose on this earth is always to help and never hinder those who need psychic intervention."

REFERENCES

PSYCHIC SYD SAEED
REFERENCE LINDA STERLING
CALIFORNIA, UNITED STATES

One has to believe Linda Sterling's first session with Syd Saeed was anything less than disheartening and disturbing, because in that very first reading the psychic revealed her son would soon be pulled over by the police and charged with drunk driving. Two weeks later he was and although Linda had wanted to connect with a true psychic who would know details about her no one else knew, she admits, this was an onerous beginning to their relationship.

"I was in a dark place with my marriage and tremendously worried about my son when I called him. Without uttering a word to Syd, he simply began to discuss in detail the concerns I had for my son and my marriage. "Other psychics with whom I had consulted were vague and disclosed generalities, such as, 'you are going to live a long life' or 'you will find happiness' when what I wanted was a person to tell me the truth and convey specifics pertinent to my life. Syd began our first session by speaking as if he had known me forever, but the truth is there was no way for me to know his first disclosure would be as negative as it was regarding my son."

Linda found Syd on the Bob Olson Best Psychic page, referred to previously, and despite the plethora of choices, he was her first choice and her last. "I will only call Syd," she affirms. "I chose him because of his excellent reviews, but equally because his appointment availability was almost immediate. Finally, I thought if he is as good as his reviews indicate then his fees are reasonable.

"I know many people who are afraid of psychics," she continues, "because they believe they are going to hear they are dying or something horrible is about to happen to them, but in reading reviews of Syd, it was obvious there were other clients, who believed his readings were factual and forthright." Even so, her anticipation of their first session was scary and Linda admits for one thing she repelled any information that would confirm she and her husband would not reconcile. However, this is precisely what Syd did reveal.

"He was adamant that if my husband and I did reconcile, it would be solely my own choice. This was true. If he had simply blurted out our relationship was over it would have been devastating, but as it was, Syd was absolutely correct because I didn't want to reconcile. I felt relieved because his gentle speaking manner absolutely gave light and softness to a difficult personal situation. "When Syd answers a telephone call from a client," Linda reveals, "he is so 'normal' you actually forget you are speaking to a stranger. He is incredibly calm and veers immediately to those issues which prompted the call in the first place. He is similar to a friend who knows a great deal about you even before you speak. Because he does, one is immediately in awe with his 'gift' but also thankful because he imparts credible information in a smooth, relaxing tone.

"My experiences prior to Syd included psychics who were slightly tempestuous and didn't want to be questioned. It seems to me they will leave clients somewhat frightened and frustrated because they do not answer the questions their clients have." She affirms her consultations with Syd rates as one of the best experiences in her life.

"I finally found a 'real' psychic, who just nails it every time I call him. You can imagine my astonishment when he cautioned me during a session to be careful because he 'felt' I was going to hurt my leg. A few months later, I did slip and break it." To Linda, psychics she consulted before Syd were fakes, and do not function as 'gifted' consultants there to help, but rather seem to act for their own gain. "Not Syd," she affirms, "he allows extra time without question and is patient when a client struggles to explain a situation." To Linda Sterling, Syd Saeed is a 'gifted' psychic, who delivers cogent guidance and support, as she lives her life. "What more can I ask for?" she concludes.

PSYCHIC SYD SAEED
REFERENCE TROY NIXON
CALIFORNIA, UNITED STATES

Question?
Does one practicing psychic seek another psychic's advice when it comes to his personal or professional life?

Answer!
Yes, he does, which is precisely why Troy Nixon who is a psychic intuitive himself, is also a faithful client of Syd Saeed. If anyone can offer logical reasons as to why a certain psychic is more precise or accurate than another, then surely Troy can offer a viable opinion.

"I wanted advice and counsel as to the best approach or direction needed to move my life forward. The answers eluded me, so I began an earnest search to find help. Of all the psychics I consulted in my search, none resonated, because the advice was either too vague or too general, or I was being told only what was thought I wanted to hear."

It might surprise readers to learn that Syd was not Troy's first choice, as he perused the Psychic Directory. In fact, Syd wasn't always listed in the directory, accordingly, he was led to many other intuitives, but was left discouraged with a feeling his needs were not being met. There was, however, another psychic with whom Troy did connect, and who did tender solid guidance which was helpful, but the relationship didn't last long.

As it happened, however, Syd and this psychic are actually colleagues who respect each other, so this recommendation and the stellar reviews by others in the profession, finally simplified Troy's choice. "To be honest," he admits, "I wanted to test his abilities and keep in mind when one is seeking advice and direction, there is bound to be a feeling of apprehension, because it is necessary to confide highly personal information then place your trust in that person so he can proffer help, and all this is done simultaneously, as you ponder your place in life."

When speaking with Syd the first time, Troy did not experience any misgivings, but actually felt relaxed and reassured. "He explained the procedures employed in his readings, and although he does not ask questions at the beginning of the session, he does allow follow-up questions before the reading ends."

"Because Syd is authentic and does not prattle away with numerous questions simply to create a storyline, he provided crucial security for me. Further, a responsible psychic does not ask questions, which for me would immediately raise a red flag."

Troy values the humour and wit Syd employs in a good way during conversations and as the sessions continued, "It is as though we had known each other all of our lives." As one psychic to another, Troy believes Syd exhibited qualities which befit a humble psychic. "He carefully ensured his visions could be immediately altered, if that was my resolve. His accuracy was astounding, and if he was off, (his word, not mine) he was never far from the truth."

Readings with Syd aren't always easy going for Troy; because the psychic continues to reveal certain characteristics about him no one but close family members know. "However, because the information emanates from this serious and caring psychic, I am open and receptive, but it is equally critical for me to believe right from the beginning, Syd endeavors to gain a client's trust and respect." Troy declares Syd is extremely precise in readings and the events he predicted did transpire after an intervening lapse of time. "I sought Syd professionally, partly because I was confused regarding a personal relationship and I also required advice regarding my career. Although Syd would deny he is accurate 100 percent of the time, in my case, I can attest he most certainly is."

Four major surgeries two years ago tested Troy physically and psychologically, and set him back professionally. He is convinced, however, the counsel Syd provides as to the best course of action to follow during his recovery, is accurate, factual and invaluable. "Help that comes when it is needed most cannot be sufficiently praised," he concludes, "and this is precisely what I get from Syd."

PSYCHIC SYD SAEED
REFERENCE RITA RICCI
ONTARIO, CANADA

Although Rita Ricci had experienced numerous readings in the past, her extensive research to find a special practitioner seemed to be fruitless, frustrating and unsatisfactory. Nonetheless, she kept searching for 'that authentic, genuine' psychic, and finally found one. "I wanted a natural but gifted reader and one who did not resort to gimmickry in his practice. The name, Syd Saeed popped up regularly, almost as though it was fate or a celestial indicator was directing me to choose him."

The Bob Olson Psychic directory was in play as Rita did her homework. "I read every testimonial which succinctly described his reputation with other clients, and once I made my decision and called, you can imagine my surprise when Syd himself answered the telephone. Destiny had intervened, so I booked an appointment, for the following day."

Curiosity, slight anxiety, but little apprehension prevailed during the first meeting, because Rita knew, almost instantly, Syd was the one psychic who would provide the guidance she sought. "I was not disappointed," she discloses, "but you must understand my skepticism because of numerous 'cold readings' I had in the past, where the so-called psychic probed or fished for information, but did not offer any direction or counsel. "Those so-called bona fide earlier psychics certainly didn't accurately 'read' or evaluate my life," Rita declares. "They lacked clear insight and offered no solutions to the issues in my life, and as do many clients who are displeased with a session, I continued to 'psychically shop around. My search ended when I met Syd."

When Syd and Rita initially connected, he made it unequivocally clear she was to reveal her name only, and must not disclose additional personal information. "An analogy," Rita laughs, "might be that of a horse race, because with rapid speed Syd used pertinent words and phrases, which precisely described my life."

Rita admits Syd continued to be 'spot on' repeatedly, as though he had a direct window into her soul. "Within five minutes," she recalls, "he reviewed my childhood, adolescence and then accurately described the relationship I have with my children and family. Syd sensed long-ago intimate memories and milestones and then discussed existing events which were precise and pertinent to my present life." What mystified Rita, no one knew these extremely private and personal details about her, but Syd did. "He also sensed the lingering skepticism and disappointment I harboured from previous readings, but they seemed to become catalysts for him to be certain he revealed only specific and precise information regarding my past. He saw! He felt! He knew! In this, I have no doubt."

Although it is difficult, Rita reveals a current serious situation presently in her life, and it is one where Syd has and will continue to be instrumental as she seeks resolution. "A grievous legal issue transpired but despite a concerted effort to locate one, or to be more precise, the 'right' lawyer to represent me I could not. After months of searching, I finally consulted Syd, who advised I would locate a young, female solicitor whose office was nearby. She will be caring, highly skilled, unequivocally professional, and she will resolve this situation," he advised.

"Talk about validation," Rita exclaims, "because soon after his prediction, I did locate a young, female lawyer, who is highly skilled and located in my community. Her vigorous representation in an ongoing defamation case is now confirmation there is light at the end of the tunnel and Syd is confident my case will be victorious. But until it is, I am gratified he continues to help me cope with the inevitable peaks and valleys." Rita affirms the compassionate, empathetic and genuine nature Syd exhibits in his readings, affirms he is a psychic who genuinely cares for his clients. "In my case, he feels what I feel and is quick to reveal the future. He will also discuss contentious issues even to describe the people involved. His cogent advice is invaluable when it reveals how I should react during these situations.

"Syd firmly believes a person's own 'free will' will conquer adversity and if desired, any situation can be changed. I am calm and at ease because of Syd who is and will be my 'go-to' psychic for guidance. It is uncanny, however, sooner or later his predictions do occur, and for me to be forewarned is to be forearmed."

What is acutely important to Rita when support and understanding from others is deficient, Syd affirms her goodness and although he will praise her when warranted, he also ensures she remains grounded and able to recognize and deal with reality. From their first meeting, Rita asserts, "Syd lit a candle in my life and has shed clarity, light and love around me. Everything with him makes sense especially regarding my family, although I admit, his revelations can also evoke anguish and distress. A year ago, during an appointment to discuss a certain matter, it was an astounding revelation when Syd, after channeling his Spirit Guide, warned me of a grievous situation that could occur within my family. Precisely one year later, a close family member struggling with overwhelming issues and problems, had reached a place where he believed his only option was to commit suicide. The complete enormity of this critical situation had eluded me, although I was aware something serious was happening. Because of Syd, our family was able to intervene and bring resolution, to a potentially painful and devastating situation."

Rita believes as Syd guides her day to day, especially in stressful incidents, she can be confident of her future. "He is an exceptional psychic/medium, who does not judge, is ethical, professional, sincere and compassionate, and best of all, he is there when I need him."

A FINAL NOTE

As you have discovered Syd Saeed wears many hats, and has worn them extremely well in his lifetime, but it is obvious his preferred choice without doubt is his role as psychic medium. He fills his days and many of his nights with clients, who come from every walk of life and it is here he obviously belongs.

As mentioned, his inclusion in this narrative came about because the story needed another dimension and additional depth, in an attempt to explain the phenomena which today is sweeping across North America. One questions if people, through psychic intervention, are seeking depth or rationale, as they deal with their complicated lives. In this, Syd seems to effectively and efficiently fill in the blanks to make living easier, or at least more palatable for them, day to day.

When I called Syd I had no idea what to expect or how he would react. Think, if it had been you, who had received a cold call from a writer you do not know, have never heard of, but one who requests you to share intimate details of your life, both personal and professional. You will remember the reaction from Syd was immediate, gracious, which confirmed without doubt, here is a man who takes his work but not himself seriously. He sits on no pedestal and does not hold himself above or beyond those of us, who do not possess his 'gift.' Rather, he feels assured what he 'sees,' 'reads,' or 'expresses' in psychic revelations is simply something he does, and is little different from everyone else, who labour in their individual professions.

His demeanour, his background, his obvious solemn and serious dedication to his clients, is perceptible. The information he receives is immediately shared with clients, but he is adamant he is not out to change a client's life, rather to enhance it. Syd continues to live his life day to day, with little deviation from a purpose which has changed little from his youth to present today. Service to others is his daily objective. It is his 'gift' and for Syd, there is no greater obligation. For those who have read Syd's Story and might like to make contact or acquire further information, you can reach him:

Telephone number: 424.888.4068 / 1.877-SYD-SAEED
Email: info@sydsaeed.com
His fees are:
$100+ per psychic reading
$100+ per medium session

Other paranormal service charges to be determined when appointment is made.

PSYCHIC

JESSICA COSTELLO
FITCHBURG,
MASSACHUSETTS
U.S.A.

AUTHOR'S NOTES

It is time I tell myself to prioritize work on the book, so despite the present preposterous pace in my life, I begin. An unforeseen event makes it more difficult at a time when this author believed the work almost finished, but it became necessary to replace a psychic I had selected for inclusion. This was a decision which necessitated a search to find another who would fit the bill, embellish and improve this story. Although there is a plethora of psychics from whom to choose, I had specific criteria in mind which dictated the person I wanted.

And I found her.

The old adage which counsels, 'We should be prepared for those times when life's vicissitudes occur unintentionally but can turn out for the best' ring incredibly true, as you might agree when you learn how I connected with Jessica Costello, natural psychic. After calling and interviewing six other paranormal operatives, some who are known, others who are not, and all of whom initially seemed to exhibit promise, it soon became apparent following consultation with each, not one of the six was a good fit. Simpatico, connection, the human link was missing and it was time to try again. Never one to give up easily, I finally went to one of the other psychics in the book for a referral, trusting this person would have contacts in the paranormal sphere, and could if he would, assist me, in my quest.

The four other psychics, whose lives are chronicled in this book, I found on my own through research or contacts, but this time perhaps because I am more aware, more cognizant of the esoteric world, in which psychics function, I couldn't seem to locate another special someone, who would appropriately round out the five.

It is an understatement to say the name given to me turned out to be not only a perfect fit, but an incredible find. She was notified in advance I would call which I did and within one day, not only did Jessica and I connect by telephone, but we also related with our minds and hearts. We seemed to interlink without effort, without planning, without design. I called, we talked, and over that weekend, we connected several more times, and to admit, Dear Reader, I am elated, is an understatement.

Please meet Jessica Costello, an internationally known Psychic, Healer, Medium, Radio Host, Wife, Mother, with a successful background in Construction Management and Engineering in her past, until, that is when her paranormal gifts would no longer be denied. Without reservations, she relinquished her professional career to begin another in the incomprehensible, supernatural world which comprises psychic phenomena. Jessica's singular credentials will be revealed as you read her story, and it is probable you will recognize here is a lady, who readily reveals her affection and connection with those who have passed on; with the benevolent Spirit world, who guide and enlighten her; and you will undoubtedly accept the belief although she is gifted in numerous paranormal spheres, perhaps her most favourite is her connection with Spirits from every walk of life, who amble aloft, ever at the ready to assist Jessica, in her readings and sessions.

Jessica's goal is to empower clients; to help them meet their goals; but also to alleviate fear and stress; and to offer hope where it is needed, along with careful and caring advice to those who seek her out, and all this is enacted with sincerity but also with a degree of insouciance and even humour. She is capable of assessing the unspoken needs of clients, even when they cannot succinctly express their own issues, and yet, she does it in such a way to assure she does not judge, diminish or belittle, the client's need for consultation.

Meet Jessica, or Jess, as she is wont to call herself, and decide for yourself if she embodies what you, the reader, would consider a true and honest psychic should be.

THE EVOLUTION OF PSYCHIC

JESSICA COSTELLO
FITCHBURG, MASSACHUSETTS

QUESTION 1

Are you a psychic medium?
  Yes, I am a medium.

QUESTION 2

Is there a difference between a psychic and a psychic medium?
  "There is a difference," Jessica explains, "all mediums are psychic, and by this I mean all mediums can give psychic intuitive guidance but not all psychics can connect to those who have passed on, as mediums do."
  She continues, "A medium is a psychic who can raise their vibrations to a frequency which allows a connection with those who have departed their physical bodies. Mediums connect with Guides and Angels, who inhabit an exceptionally high frequency," which is why Jessica concludes, "most people cannot see or hear them."

QUESTION 3A

At what age did you discover you had this wonderful but supernatural gift?
  "Tough question!" Jessica exclaims, "because I have been speaking with the dead for as long as I can remember, but it did not dawn on me this was unusual

or that other people did not 'see' as I did until I was about six years old." She remembers when she would try to discuss a psychic friend or a ghostly animal pal with others, that despite how real these specters were to her, she was simply told she had a vivid imagination.

Jessica admits she honestly believed all kids were as she was and also enjoyed these same spectral friendships. It didn't occur to her these apparitions she considered to be friends, were undetectable to others. "I saw auras everywhere even at a young age, but I thought they were people's shadows and clearly visible to everybody. I can still recall being embarrassed and shocked when it became evident to me these spirits were not shadows and were undetectable to other people."

QUESTION 3B

Did your mother or father know you were so 'gifted,' and if so, did they ever advise you, when you were young, to keep this 'gift' to yourself?

Jessica's mother was reluctant to recognize or traverse the paranormal road her young daughter travelled, and when her daughter attempted to talk about the apparitions she envisioned, her mother would simply tell her she was incredibly smart, bright and inventive, perhaps somewhat unusual too, but nonetheless, she would exclaim, those visions were simply an offshoot of her vivid imagination.

"Even as a kid," Jessica reveals, "I would take an immediate like or dislike to certain people and I did not understand why. I remember refusing to visit a certain house during Halloween, when we were out trick or treating, and although I had neither met nor spoken to the people who lived in that dwelling, I simply would not cross their property."

Much later, she learned they were heavy drug dealers and it was later still when Jessica understood it was their vibrations which had so negatively affected her. She adds, "When I would tell my mom I knew specific facts about someone I didn't know, she would tell me that it was 'verboten' to tell wild stories about people. Amazingly, even when my revelations turned out to be true, my poor mom never did connect the dots. She did not want to." Jessica admits it may sound strange today to confess in her younger years, she would take immediate like or dislike to certain colleagues of her parents, and would go so far as to warn her parents not to do business with them. What is still amazing to her all these years later, is recognizing her mother still does not accept how she perceived they were unethical, despite events which unequivocally proved otherwise, especially in business dealings.

She is thankful her father was more receptive to these admonitions and when he would enquire how, "I knew or where the information originated, I would simply respond it came to me from my psychic pipeline. I was incredibly serious, but my Dad, who would listen, never did fully understand.

"On the other hand," Jessica admits, "I was also a kid who would warm up to people who others may not like." She remembers a colleague of her parents whom others thought to be crusty and obnoxious. "I did not see him in that way and despite my mother's warning he was 'the meanest man on earth,' I worked for him immediately after high school and during that time, I still did not witness these characteristics in him. I got to know a sweet, if grouchy man, who possessed a sarcastic sense of humour, but was also a person who, when he needed an employee, was willing to hire me despite my young age, regardless of the fact numerous applicants wanted the job. I was a girl to boot, but I was the one he hired." It turns out Jessica was vindicated in her opinion of this man because "he was a 'blast' to work for, and was both kind and good to me."

When older, as she tried to explain her 'gift' to her parents, she admits all those times in her youth when she was actually 'seeing things' and knew they were not a product of her imagination as her mother would insist, "the admonition still stings when I remember mom telling me that 'schizophrenia' can set in at any time." Thus it is even today the challenge of being accepted by her family as pertains to her 'gift' continues.

"I was raised by two civil engineers/land surveyors whose early design for me was to grow up, get educated and clone what they did." Given their pragmatic backgrounds, Jessica can now easily appreciate how difficult it was for them to grasp anything that did not have a formula or equation attached to it. "This ensured both my parents tap-danced around my 'knowing things' and when I mentioned seeing Spirits in my room as a little child, my mother would tell me I was hallucinating, give me an aspirin and send me to bed. Ergo; I learned early on and quickly although my parents were wonderful resources on many levels, they did not recognize my psychic abilities were realistic or genuine."

QUESTION 4A

Apart from knowing you had the 'gift' what were you like as a child?

This question prompts an immediate response from Jessica, who asserts she was just like any other kid. "Well," she admits, "almost, although I did know I was different too. I did not have a ton of friends and being around many people tended to be overwhelming for me. But what ensured I would be even more alone, was then and still is the fact I have no tolerance for people who are not themselves or who try to be something they are not.

"In a high school setting," she says, "most students simply try to fit in, ignore their own uniqueness, and do what they perceive must be done to become part of the pack." Jessica remembers she found more comfort in hanging out with her animals and had 'tons' of pets to enjoy, including a cat and dog with whom she could play and cuddle. "I have talked to animals very likely since birth and connect with them more readily even now than I do with people." Jessica recalls a traumatic event when cows on the family's farm were slated for a trip to the abattoir. She begged and pleaded with her parents and grandfather to allow the one with whom she had bonded to be spared, but her pleas fell on deaf ears. To this day she believes animals know in advance when their time is up. "I hated that," she recalls.

She admits, as a teenager, in some ways she was typical and as such, she was snotty, mouthy, and thought her parents were 'dumb, dumb, dumb.' She simply wanted to be normal. "Normal to me meant doing all of the things other teens did such as attending parties and dances and it didn't occur to me then my own behaviour was responsible for the obstacles I encountered, in my quest to be accepted by and involved with other teens.

"Being a teenager is rough on any psychic," she opines, "and although hormones, angst, and altering moods can affect anyone, for a sensitive they seem to be even more agitating, because you are not dealing with just you, you are contending with those Spirits, who surround and intervene constantly in your daily life." It requires little insight to recognize her teen years were a challenge for Jessica, who admits reviving certain incidents can still evoke melancholy and sadness for her simply in the remembering.

QUESTION 4B

Was your childhood ever affected positively or negatively by the 'gift?'

"I would say both," Jessica admits. "On the one hand I was one of those kids who could ace a test and even as a college student, I could neglect opening a book for the entire term and still score a 97 as a final grade. I simply knew the answers." What she confesses now might even today be chilling for her teachers because she recalls instinctively knowing certain personal things about teachers, 'stuff' that was not public knowledge, and she also 'knew' facts about her peers and their families, which was not general knowledge.

"When I was in the seventh grade, I met a fellow student who was disliked by almost everyone, although she and I formed a friendship. After we became friends, I had a vision of her older brother as he forced her to endure inappropriate acts. It troubled me enormously to the point I told my mother what I had sensed. Mother admonished and warned me not to speak about this to anyone because people would judge me to be to be no better than those I criticized. In other words, my mother believed I too, would be called a pervert." Regardless of her mother's admonition, Jessica could not let the vision go. Her concern manifested to the point she had no choice but intervene in this situation in any way she could. "I asked the young lady, who is now my friend, to stay at my house at night, which she did for the entire summer. Sadly, by the end of the season, it was time for her go home, despite the obvious reasons that had kept her away.

"That dreadful day," Jessica recalls, "we both hid in the attic until we were finally discovered, and it isn't difficult to imagine the incredible drama that ensued as two 'tweens' intent on hiding from adults, had to explain their outlandish behaviour. I remember it was difficult for my parents to accept my vision, which helped me to recognize being different had both an up and a downside. It also meant I had few friends, although those I did have were incredibly special to me. Despite parental criticism or displeasure, my loyalty to a 'friend' was vitally important to me, regardless of circumstance or consequence."

Amazingly, it was only recently Jessica reconnected with her friend by way of Facebook. This same lady, not well liked in her youth, is still beset with difficulties as happiness and a successful relationship with men is impaired, because of those early childhood experiences. She has two children but confided to Jessica despite the fact men find her attractive, she is most content within herself or in the company of children and friends. As a nurse, she has found purpose and independence in life, and is confident their renewed friendship will provide her continued support and sustenance. She is confident Jessica will be there when needed because this is what friends are for.

QUESTION 4C

Did other children recognize you were different?

"Oh my! Oh my! They certainly did," concedes Jessica, "but they did not know what it was that made me different. I certainly did not reveal to them I talked to dead people all the time, or I knew all about their 'secret Star Trek' addiction, or that they might have a hidden crush on someone. Oh, no indeed, I did not do this for such revelations would have ensured my isolation to an even greater degree than it already was."

Jessica kept her insights to herself because her mother constantly advised her it was taboo to discuss such things in public. "I doubt the other kids knew the reason why I had the ability to do well in school without studying or exerting any effort, and I am certain as with other psychic children, I was a loner not necessarily by choice but by necessity."

QUESTION 4D

What were your teen years like?

"Horrible and wonderful! Certainly, I went through all the stuff everyone else did, but I had the added challenge of dealing with the energy of those unnamed others, who were ever present in my life." Jess remembers during her rebellious stage she seemed to get away with any behaviour that happened along. If my parents were going out, I could spend the time watching television, talking on the phone, simply goofing off, because I knew the exact time they would be home. I ensured the house was spiffy and I was at the books, for indeed, I was indeed, the model child."

Jessica believes she was one of the best babysitters in town because she knew exactly what the kids would do and when. She recalls sitting with three adorable but precocious children no one else would attend, but who for her were easily managed and well behaved. "I knew prior to their naughty moves what they were about to do, and when I would mention it, those poor kids clearly could not understand how or why I would know."

QUESTION 5

How did the revelation that you possessed this 'gift' make itself evident to you?

"When I was eleven or twelve, my baby brother became desperately ill," Jessica remembers, "my parents had diagnosed the illness as a virulent stomach bug, but they were worried enough to take him to the doctor, but I was left home alone to do the laundry. We had just moved to Maine and were living in a house once occupied by a wonderful older lady with whom I had enjoyed a lovely relationship. I would regularly visit and help her around the house, and after she passed away that year my parents rented her home, while our own house was being built.

"I loved that woman so much," Jessica recounts, and speaks of the time when she was hanging clothes on the line outside when the deceased lady appeared. "How could this be I wondered? I had attended her funeral. I knew she was dead, yet, there she was, as substantial as she had been in life. She had a message for me and acknowledged my brother was extremely ill but soon my parents would telephone to say he would undergo immediate surgery, remain in hospital for a week, and then come home to recover completely. "Further," she advised, "because I was terribly frightened she would stay with me until my parents returned. Less than a half hour later my parents did call to describe my brother's situation exactly as 'Spirit Lady' had predicted. My mother's fear was obvious and she said nothing more, but I did not, could not, tell her about my dead friend's presence and prediction, or why when everyone else was on edge and agitated, I was calm and certain my brother would be well again. I knew instinctively my mother would not understand nor would she accept such esoteric predictions.

"That long day while I waited for my parents to return, my Spirit friend stayed with me, and spoke of her long deceased husband. She taught me how to make 'hermit cookies' which I still make to this day (and which I declare are tastier than those made by my mother.) The presence of this steady, quiet Spirit along with her revelations, once again substantiated I was different indeed, but what was even more astounding, was the realization that just as I could see and hear the dead, so could they see and hear me." 'Spirit Lady' appeared once again to Jessica later that same year to prepare her for the impending loss of her beloved old dog, Jake. She advised her not be upset or angry with her parents because they were that day to take Jake to the veterinarian where, because he was old and suffering, a decision would be made to end his life. She said to give Jake an extra hug and cuddle that morning before I left for school and say goodbye.

Jessica remembers her disbelief when her parents did not discuss these dismal plans with her, but she said nothing to them of the Spirit Lady, who had appeared the night before. "I petted and played with my dog as usual that morning, but I also remember glaring at my father over breakfast willing him to 'come clean' but he did not. I was later told that Jake had gone outside to lie down, could not get up, and was taken to the vet, never to return. At least, I had an opportunity to say goodbye," she concludes, "because my dead Spirit friend had prepared me for this traumatic event."

QUESTION 6

What was your first experience in this field?

Jessica wonders if this question refers to the time when she is actually working in the field or just being psychic, but replies accordingly.

"I have decided to reveal both events," she declares. "My first working experience involved the healing of a young woman, who suffered with chronic, excruciating pain over a long time. It was unusual for me to travel to a reading because even now I seldom leave my home, however, the special needs in this case left me little choice. Irregular as it was, I also carried my tools and supplies, in preparation for whatever might occur.

"Once there and during the entire healing process, I recognized there was a Spirit woman with me who would continually offer psychic advice as to what I should do and how to do it. She indicated if I would follow her precise advice this healing would succeed. But talk about a plethora of unsolicited information," Jessica laughs, "because this Spirit never ceased to chatter. She suggested we learn if the client had difficulty sleeping through the night which she did, but we also discovered this was only part of her immediate problem. So much of her pain emanated from sleep deprivation, partly because she had a lively young child, who demanded attention day and night.

"The client also worked full time in a demanding job which also zapped her daily strength," Jessica recalls, "but as the healing process continued, "I became aware her Grandmother Spirit had joined us. She said her granddaughter had made several misguided life choices in the past, all of which were contributing to her present insomnia and stress." Grandmother Spirit demanded Jessica tell her granddaughter what she revealed and what was more compelling was her conviction that until her granddaughter addressed these issues, her rest and general health would be negatively affected.

For Jessica, the more positive aspect of this healing, was the appearance of Spirit Grandmother, who was able to isolate the main source of distress and trouble. "Her cogent advice that if her granddaughter would change her ways the pain would end, and I hope she did."

Jessica admits her first psychic experience is slightly more difficult to nail down, but recalls an event which happened when she was still a youngster. She was sent away to visit a member of her family and while there, had several sad dreams about her little 'kitty cat,' Bonnie, who in the recurring dreams, was dying. Strangely, after the third time, Jessica learned her cat had died and further, her parents had replaced her 'Bonnie' with another they also named 'Bonnie.' Once home, Jessica innately knew, although her parents said nothing, this cat was different. "Its voice was dissimilar, as were her mannerisms and it seemed to be constantly 'introducing' herself to me. Why in the world I wondered, why would my cat of three years do this? I knew she wouldn't and despite the fact the new 'Bonnie' looked like the original, I knew it was not her.

"Finally, my mother confessed my 'Bonnie' had escaped the house, ran into the street, was hit by a car and died, and although we kept her replacement and called her, 'Bonnie Number Two,' I wasn't duped because Spirit, who spoke to me in those dreams, ensured I was well prepared in advance for the events ahead."

QUESTION 7

Do you remember things before, as, or after they happen, or all of the above? If you can give an example(s) of each that would be beneficial.

Jessica responds, "all of the above and then describes multiple occasions when she 'sees' something before it happens. "Why just last week, I was house cleaning and thinking I would stay up later than usual to watch a movie. It was then a vision revealed my 11:00 a.m. client for the next day would arrive early at 9:45 a.m. and if she did, then typically I would be rushing around preparing my special working place, so the movie was out and I spent the time setting up for the session. This meant I had time for a leisurely tea break before the reading, and you guessed it. My client arrived over an hour early, but thanks to my 'vision' I was relaxed and ready, which is important because if I am unhurried, I can then my serve my clients with absolute tranquility."

Jessica pauses to say she often dreams about incidents which will happen the following day and with sadness remembers every pet she had that passed away. "I always knew the night before because of my dreams. In them, I am greeted by my old dog, Jake, who would be playing with one of my pets, but then, came to me as if to tell me, he would be there to greet each one and care for them when they passed."

If Jessica is psychically 'viewing' a situation for a client she can envision events as they are playing out. For example, she relates an occasion when she was checking into a work situation for a client. "I was able to see beyond what she had already realized for herself, and confirmed there was serious tension in the office setting. Not only did I 'see' the present situation, but more critical was where my client would be in six months, a year, and even two years hence.

"It was an extremely stressful time for her because the company had recently restructured their management team and my client was uncertain as to how she would fit in or if her position in the company was secure. Because my psychic 'gift' allowed me this 'insight,' I counselled my client to structure her work to favour her. Immediately, the stress diminished, the situation at work resolved in her favour and life was so much improved, exactly as I had predicted."

Jessica refers to a friend who was the mother of a 13-year-old daughter. This child was extremely challenging to raise, and Jessica could not stop the images of the girl which appeared regularly to her. Psychically, she would 'see' the young lady skipping school, sneaking out of the house, or getting involved in even more egregious behavior.

These projections appeared to Jess on the very nights they occurred which she then shared with the mother. The revelations stopped the young lady in her tracks, but they were not the most pleasant of visions, Jess opines.

In another instance, Jess recounts she is often awakened by a Spirit who seems always to be around. "One evening, he shared a psychic scene with me wherein two men were breaking into our home. I knew the time, the car they would be driving, and where it would be parked the while the thieves performed their nefarious deeds. All this I was shown before it occurred as a warning from my Spirit Friend, who wanted my husband and me to be on guard. And we were! Sure enough, the attempted robbery occurred as predicted, but the thieves were caught in the act. It was interesting to say the least when I tried to explain to the attending police officer as to how I knew precisely what would happen before it actually did." Jessica can 'see' incidents from the past, but even more disturbing are the times when she will shake someone's hand, and is instantly aware of events from their past, sometimes good, other times not. She can enter a person's home when instantly her mind's eye will 'envision' every single person who ever lived in that home. "It is disconcerting to say the least, because I can clearly picture incidents as they happened in the past." Jessica believes these events are revealed to her so she will have a more clear understanding as to why clients make choices that seem to be fraught with trouble. "My revelations help me to better help them," she affirms.

QUESTION 8

Have you ever been incorrect in your readings?

"Of course!" Jessica declares. "We are all wrong now and then and it is certain no one is 100 per cent correct all the time. One might think they are, but if a psychic is so inclined," she says, "it is time to evaluate why, because most emphatically, it cannot be.

"However," she continues, "as the question pertains to my own psychic life, it is important to recognize in getting messages from Spirit or if I receive them intuitively, the meanings might not always be clearly stated or understood. Then again," according to Jessica, "one does have to interpret the messages, which means errors can and are made."

She cautions when psychics are dealing with predictions, it is wise to remember the free will of the client can profoundly impact the outcome of foretold events, which can alter the end result. "This same energy emanates from free will and dwells in each and every person."

QUESTION 9

What, if any, was your worst, most scary or negative experience when using your 'gift?'

Without pausing, Jessica relates this story:

"A number of years ago we were living in a profoundly haunted house, a place where no one else would continue to reside for even six months, and yet, we lasted three years but not without incidents." She recalls it was a constant battle to balance the energy in the place, to keep it under control and clearly remembers a day when she came out of the bathroom, to encounter a particular Spirit, who remained her constant companion despite her attempt to ignore him.

"He told me to leave immediately for my mother's home but I wasn't about to take a three-hour drive and I am not given to 'pop-in' visits, so I declined and ignored him. In no time he appeared again, but this time he advised even more urgently I go to the grocery store. Again I declined, ignored him, and went into the bedroom and in a defiant gesture, picked up a book. Within minutes I was pushed down on the bed and harshly shaken by a strong and intense Spirit energy. "Although I finally pushed the energy away the message was clear. I must leave the house immediately and I did.

"Within minutes I was about a mile up the road when I witnessed a horrific, fatal motorcycle accident, the sight of which sent me rushing back home again." It is here Jessica's recollection takes on an eerie context and one difficult to believe, but when she entered the house to address the Spirit who had verbally assaulted her, she discovered the Spirit had reincarnated into the man who had moments before, been killed in the motorbike accident.

How can this be, you ask, Dear Reader? Jessica explains it this way. "To Spirits, who hover all around me," she says, "I stick out like a sore thumb because as a psychic I can see, hear and feel their presence. The man from the accident had been in a state of terror when he passed, and because I was in close proximity to him at that time, he was drawn to me."

Jessica used the word attack to describe their encounter, but in retrospect she now believes he was not dangerous rather he only trying to get her attention to help him. "He meant me no harm whatsoever, and simply wanted someone to understand and comfort him, through what was a horrifying ordeal." The next incident occurred about six months later, when she was struck with an excruciating headache. It was painful but also awkward because a client was soon to arrive for a reading. "The pain was incredibly intense and unlike any I had previously experienced. I was inclined to cancel the reading, but with the client almost at the door, doing so was impossible. Once we sat down together the pain intensified," Jessica recalls, but the explanation for the headache suddenly became clear."

Jessica immediately envisioned a man being shot in the head and the graphic images of gore and blood manifested in the vision and were as authentic as though the chance event was happening right then. She quickly realized the man she envisioned in the scene was her client's brother and explains, Spirits will often come to her hours, days or even weeks before a client will call her for an appointment.

Why?

How?

Read on! "I am an empath," she asserts. "I felt the brother's pain and was shown his moment of death in an immediate and vivid way. It was horrifying but what I couldn't determine why he needed to show me such grotesque details. I knew his sister had never indulged in a reading before this one and was an admitted skeptic, so it may well have been her brother wanted to ensure his sister would know exactly what had happened to him. Perhaps he simply wanted me to understand what he had endured at the time of his death, but either/or," Jessica concludes, "it was for me a profoundly intense and chilling experience."

QUESTION 10

Do you have a favourite or most memorable session?

"I have so many favourites," Jessica responds, "but I think the one that stands out happened a few weeks ago, and crazy as this may sound, this is a true and honest recollection of events.

"I was on the phone with a client and as we reviewed incidents in her life, we began to hone onto a specific event, when suddenly, I started to itch like crazy. Every inch of my skin felt as though it was covered in bug bites, which continued until finally I recognized the cause. I told my client, although she was reluctant to change the subject, it was apparent she had a severe case of poison ivy and immediately needed to take a hot baking soda bath. Further," Jessica said, "it will be necessary for you to miss work tomorrow."

Despite her surprise, the client admitted the rash had appeared the day before and was so irritable she had actually made an appointment with her doctor for a steroid injection. Jessica found it hilarious only moments before the itch hit, she had been discussing the client's love life with her. "You might say," Jennifer laughs, "the love bug bit me, but the session gave both of us an enormous laugh, although it ended in a surprising fashion."

In another example, Jessica recalls a session when she was discussing certain upcoming, romantic dates a client had arranged with a suitor. This girl's Spirit Aunt appeared in the reading to indicate how much she liked the young man and insisted on singing his praises. Spirit Aunt also insisted Jessica tell her niece she was not allowed to wear the usual plain black dress on the date with the young man, then proceeded to describe the dress the client should wear. "It will be found," Spirit Aunt continued, "in the back of the closet hanging on the right side."

What was more even more shocking and somewhat confusing to Jessica occurred when Spirit Aunt continued speaking to her niece with advice to burn all of the clothes on the left side of the closet because they made her look like a librarian. "This was the Spirit's comparison, not mine," Jessica quickly adds.

"Spirit Aunt was exceedingly blunt and extremely sassy," Jessica remembers, "as she insisted her niece 'vamp up' for her dates." Both she and the client laughed uproariously at the spectral advice which emanated from a Spirit, who possessed an apparent and singular fashion sense, and who wasn't the least bit reluctant to render unearthly advice.

QUESTION 11

How do you acquire your clients?

Jessica reveals although she is registered with a few psychic directories which do provide some new clients, she also keeps a record as to how clients do become acquainted with her services. By last count, she affirms, approximately 60 per cent are referrals from previous clients.

QUESTION 12

Can you, as a psychic, manipulate a person for whom you are doing a reading?

"Manipulate, as in mind control," she ponders, and then emphatically replies, "no! not ever! All I do is share information, insight and pass on messages, from those who have crossed over."

QUESTION 13

Is there ever a time or with a certain kind of person when your 'gift' does not work, and if so, why would this be?

"Mmmmm, sure," Jessica discloses, "there are certainly times when I can't connect with someone. It has happened a few times and further, there are also times when someone addicted to psychics and have several readings on a regular basis with any number of them are wise they don't petition me for one, because all I would hear are sounds similar to radio static. It is also clear these specific clients don't follow productive advice anyway, so there is no point arranging a session, and I am equally grateful I receive advanced knowledge about them, because it ensures we will not meet."

Jessica remembers an instance of a few years ago when a man booked a session with her and paid by cheque. "I had an extremely bad feeling about him," she recalls, "but despite my misgivings and because he was incredibly polite and kind, I went ahead and arranged a reading. As it turned out, my regular Spirit contacts would not participate and I received no messages. Not one," she emphasizes, "and believe me, I have since learned this is a red flag in the psychic world. "If the dead do not want to associate with someone there is a reason," she continues, "and during his session, two Spirits with whom I have connections finally did appear. They lingered throughout the sitting but offered no reply to each and every question the client asked, which meant I could not provide intuitive answers. Spirits must verbalize psychically to me before I can speak, and when they finally did their advice was exceedingly bad. It took tremendous energy on my part to push these two Spirits away and ignore their bizarre comments before I could continue to work with the man.

"Somehow I finished the session," Jessica declares, "I answered all his questions, after which he asked for a Reiki healing session. For me to comply it is imperative the client and I must be vibrationally matched, but before we could begin the two Spirits popped back in again and one yelled, 'No! Oh hell, no! He is treating you like a (expletive) hole. He needs to leave… now!'"

If you, Dear Reader, are somewhat taken aback that Spirits will use profanity, Jessica reveals they will and readily do, especially if they want her attention. She concludes a Spirit, 'colourful' in life, will emit off-colour language in their apparitional form, "If that is what it takes to be heard." Jessica knows her task was to listen and pay close attention when 'Spirit Peter' spoke to her. He advised she give this client 'the boot' but immediately have his payment cheque certified. "Sure enough," she exclaims, "the cheque was written on an account long since closed and further, he had 'fleeced' several other business and individuals over the previous year.

"I had a bad feeling when he came in," she admits, "but I didn't want to hurt his feelings by turning him away. My two Spirits, by being a general nuisance and interfering in the session, did everything they could to discourage me from working with him, but I ignored their psychic advice. Initially," she remembers, "I was annoyed to say the least with their astonishing behaviour, but now I not only appreciate what they did, but I can laugh at how they did it."

QUESTION 14

Do you control your psychic power or does it have authority over you?

"Both!" Jessica replies, "there are certainly times when I can shut myself down and ignore Spirit impressions or messages. In fact," she admits, "if I could not control the 'gift' I would be up a tree or in a nuthouse a long time ago. Being able to shut down and go back to simply being a wife, parent or friend is exceedingly important to any intuitive."

She admits 'closing down' is vital to one's own physical health, but that being said," Jessica continues, "there are times when I completely shut off to attend to personal business, but still be slammed with a psychic impression. When this occurs it is generally a warning.

"When these alerts manifest," she continues, "they often foretell something bad is about to happen and I am then instantly aware of a palpable bad smell and an unpleasant taste in my mouth. The air will take on an unpleasant odour and the taste in my mouth becomes acidic bile. This has happened several times and it is extremely unnerving."

Jessica admits when these signs occur, instinctively she knows something terrible will occur but what is even more frustrating and frightening is the recognition she can do nothing to stop it. The following example clearly illustrates what she means.

"The morning of the Boston Marathon bombing my husband and I had both taken the day off from work. The children were visiting my mother for a week out of state and we were lounging in bed, contemplating what we would do with this delightful, but rather unusual free time, set aside just for us.

"Parents, who seldom have such options, will completely understand children and work free days rarely occur and we certainly wanted to take advantage of our 'couple time' and have some fun. As we began to plan our day that terrible smell suddenly hit me, followed by the acrid taste in my mouth and all I could think was, 'oh no!'

"Every time we considered leaving the house for our special time together, the symptoms worsened until finally we realized the day we had planned was not to be. We stayed home and it was only a few hours later when news of the bombing hit the airwaves."

Jessica instantly remembered it was only a week before she had a dream about explosions but thought they were simply an aftermath of a science fiction movie she had watched before going to bed. "Suddenly," she affirms, "it was clear the indicators she experienced were horrifying omens and a clear indication of this disaster. Sadly, there was nothing I could do to help avert this tragedy."

Jessica discloses as a medium, she is frequently connected to Spirits who want her to do something singular for them. They may want me to convey a message to someone or make contact for whatever reason which can be incredibly overwhelming. "I can tune them out the same way I would stop background noise emanating from a radio or television located in another room, but it is not always a simple thing to do." She concludes, however, if she tuned in every Spirit who finds his or her way unannounced or uninvited into her space, she is certain her head would have exploded years ago.

QUESTION 15

Do you consider your psychic power a 'gift' or a 'curse?'

Again, Jessica's reply is an instantaneous 'both.' She explains it is a 'gift' to help people and she loves the feeling of peace she gains from knowing there is something beyond this physical life. "It is a blessing to connect with Spirit as easily as I do, but I also absolutely love the fact I can also 'see' my grandmother every single day and be assured she is with my children when they go to bed.

"She passed away when I was five, but there is never a day when she does not emerge to say hello. I get to talk with her and other than my son, I am the only person in my family to have this special connection. She was a medium in her lifetime, which means she has a special interest in me and knowing we have this bond is deeply comforting." Jessica recalls the time a few years ago when her father's friend passed only to have him appear to her to ask a favour. "It was a bit odd," she recalls, "but his Spirit took residence in my space and for over six months, he was never more than three feet away from me. It was a trifle creepy to have my dad's friend hanging out in my bedroom every night, so I finally relented and agreed to do what he wanted.

"Since then, he has maintained a decent distance, and only pops in now and then to offer a sarcastic remark or warn me about something about to occur. It may sound odd," she states, "but I rather enjoy this Spirit now, as he is just plain fun and means no harm or danger to me or mine."

Jessica concludes, however, psychic insight can also be a 'curse,' especially when she personally feels the pain or suffering a Spirit has endured in life. "It can be equally debilitating and exceedingly sad to visualize the sorrow certain people experience in their lifetime, some of which may also cling to them after death."

QUESTION 16

Do you summon your 'gift' or does it have a will of its own?

"If I am being warned something is about to happen," Jessica discloses, "then the 'gift' has a will of its own, and no amount of trying to tune it out will stop the information from coming through to me. But it is unnecessary to summon psychic vision to receive a message," she admits, "for if I simply stop interfering or tune out, there it is unbidden and at times unwanted."

Jessica does admit again nevertheless, there are times for the benefit of her own health and wellness, when she does tune out, although she will still receive impressions. "I release them rather than tuning in, because I can always go back to them later." She concludes, "Doing this is akin to taking a telephone message to return the call later on."

The writer is convinced Jessica's psyche is one busy place inhabited by so many Spirits, one wonders how she keeps her sanity with so many occupants invading her space. But wonder aside; on to the next question.

QUESTION 17

How do strangers react to you when you encounter them? Do they have any idea or realization that you have the 'gift?'

"I don't disclose this information to strangers I meet in public," Jessica affirms. "I am just like every other mother, wife or friend when I am out and about in my personal life. I am a rather private person in that sense and people generally only know of my paranormal life when they come to me for psychic services, or if they hear about me from others."

Jessica has experienced several occasions, however, when someone will recognize her from an event she has attended, or will have previous knowledge as to who she is. They may then approach her and begin to ask questions. "I have been at parties with friends," she conveys, "when one of the other guests will reveal who I am and what I do, and it is then I am deluged with people all of whom have questions about their lives and futures, or often too, regarding their loved ones who have passed."

Although she is gratified to be well received by other folks, she will frequently manage such situations by simply advising she is not working at that particular time and is therefore, tuned out.

QUESTION 18

Once people are aware you are 'gifted' or have psychic powers, do they react with:
    Skepticism?
    "Of course! But it is understandable if a person has no experience with a psychic, it will be difficult for them to comprehend how one person can 'see' something that most others cannot."
    Fear?
    "Yup! That too," Jessica exclaims. "I have worked with people who react with fear, but again, it is usually because they are still unsure about what it is that

psychics do. Also, it is true some people with deep religious views will assume because I am a psychic, I am in cahoots with the devil. For the most part, this attitude is simply due to lack of knowledge which can generate a lack of acceptance. This doesn't occur frequently, but it has happened in the past. One simply has to work through it."

Disbelief?

"All the time!" Jessica explains. "Every single day I meet with someone who disbelieves I can know the things I know about them. This is also true when I relate numerous details about one of their dead relatives, and reveal specifics, such as name, date of death, cause of death, career path, how many children they had and what they loved or hated in life. It can be difficult for a person to believe, because there I am sitting with them 'talking away' rather normally, with someone I can 'see' but they cannot."

People also react with curiosity, excitement and exhilaration, she affirms and mentions those times when she is at a function with her children when someone will reveal to others she is a psychic medium, ("they never learn this from me") and once this information is out the questions immediately begin. It is merely an offset of the person she is and Jessica is well adjusted to the paradigm she generates.

QUESTION 19

Do your psychic powers ever get you into trouble?

"Not really," Jessica affirms, "although I remember another time which occurred a few years ago. We were having issues with a couple of people (those same two teenagers) who had earlier broken into our home but fled, when they realized I was home and had called the police.

Here, Jessica interrupts herself to remind Readers of the earlier incident when two youths tried to break into her home. "Despite the fact we lived in a small town it was egregious as to the length of time it took the police to respond to my call. They were certainly too late to investigate the incident."

There was another attempt but on this occasion Jessica was ready because of the 'gift.'

"I was in bed when a message was transmitted from Spirit, who revealed a green Toyota 4Runner occupied by two males would park down the street at

2:39 a.m. and then cut through the woods to break into the garage. I set the alarm for 2:00 a.m. called the police at 2:30 a.m. just before the event was predicted to occur. Sure enough the police arrived at exactly the same time as did the would-be thieves, so the robbery was thwarted." Jessica recalls it was challenging later when she tried to explain to the police officers as to how she was able to call them before the crime took place. The potential robbers were the same two boys, who had previously tried to rob her home and who had also committed similar intrusions at other homes in the vicinity. "There are times," Jessica admits, "when explaining the 'gift' is complicated and will raise doubt and curiosity.

QUESTION 20

Do doors that would normally be difficult to enter, open for you because of your psychic powers?

"Not really," muses Jessica. "Well, not anymore but in my previous career, I did excel during the interview process. I was able to envision details about a job opportunity, so consequently I could prepare for it in advance. I never went to a job interview where I was not offered the position and at the risk of appearing arrogant, I have always been exceedingly adept at communicating with all different personality types. I am fortunate because intuitively, I can connect with people on a level familiar and comfortable for them, which in turn ensures they will readily respond to me."

QUESTION 21

Are you a healer and what is your definition of a healer?

"I am a healer," Jessica declares, "and my definition of a healer is someone who extends healing whether it is physical or spiritual. Of course, doctors and nurses are healers who use medicine to heal, but I am a 'Lightworker' and in this, I use energy to heal."

In her 'practice' she uses Reiki, Crystal Healing, Herbal Therapy, Aroma Therapy and many other forms of healing. "In each healing session," she continues, "I tune in intuitively to my client to decide what method will be best suited for the person with whom I am working. My energy and psychic powers also aid me as I detect those issues that provoke or disturb my client."

Jessica exclaims she never charges a fee when she employs her healing skills. "It is reward enough if I can help heal a person's physical body and it is my 'path' to do this regardless of someone's ability to pay."

QUESTION 22

How do you control your 'gift' or does it need to be controlled?

"I meditate for no less than two hours every day. I must because meditation helps me to shut down and ensure I will not become overwhelmed with psychic impressions as I live my daily life." But having said this, Jessica admits she has yet to figure out how to block Spirits from contact in her chosen off-hours. "When I am intentionally tuned out for rest time and a Spirit approaches me as they frequently do, I simply ignore them.

"Meditation and shutdown time is key for me," she continues, "otherwise, I cannot walk through a grocery store without visions concerning every single person I pass. They crowd my psyche."

Jessica explains, "Intuition is like a muscle, the more you use it, the stronger it gets, ergo; after a long work week if I do not mediate to close my day, it is analogous to a radio that brings in all of the channels of the world, but all at the same time."

QUESTION 23

Is psychic power the same as intuitive power?

"In my opinion, without any doubt, it is," she replies.

QUESTION 24

Can the 'gift' be misused?

"Yes! Yes it can, and unfortunately, it often is," Jessica laments. "Often, indeed too many times, I will witness even ethical psychics use their 'gifts' inappropriately, and it profoundly troubles me.

"This can occur when a psychic might tune into a person's insecurities, prey on them, and provide inaccurate information, during a reading. Further," she adds, "if psychics 'read' someone without invitation or permission, it is a serious and blatant misuse of their energy."

QUESTION 25

Is it possible for one with the 'gift' to become arrogant in having it?

Her emphatic reply! "ALL! THE! TIME!"

Jessica continues her unequivocal response by observing, "On a daily basis, I am in contact with psychics, who are so full of themselves they are an obvious embarrassment to ethical healers and intuitives everywhere. The press and media these days promote and run television programs about the paranormal and mediums because people are more curious and interested in life after death, in psychics and in the unearthly.

"Many psychics get caught up in that hype and become so full of themselves," she continues, "they become a shell of the 'Lightworker' they were." For Jessica, this situation both saddens and troubles her because she believes those who have the 'gift,' also have an obligation to use it honestly and honourably.

QUESTION 26

Because you believe your 'gift' comes from God, can it be purloined by the devil or evil forces?

Jessica's immediate reply is 'no,' not in her case because she believes her Guides protect her from all lower vibrational energy, which can manifest as 'evil beings.'

"If I miss the warning, my Guides will ensure I experience a most painful headache, which is an indication for me to be on guard and immediately terminate any relationship that could be brewing with an entity, whose sole purpose is malevolent."

QUESTION 27

Fanciful as this question is, what is heaven like as envisioned by a psychic?

Jessica sees heaven as a place where one will encounter unconditional love from family and Spirit. "It is a place where loved ones who are departed, wait to guide and assist each one of us through an eventual transition and enlightenment." Although she is perfectly happy and content here on Earth, she also believes, "Heaven to be a true paradise and it is there for all humanity."

QUESTION 28

How many hours per week do you use your paranormal powers?

Jessica quickly admits it is impossible for her to read for more than and often less than 40 hours a week or "My head would explode and my nerves would snap." On average, she reads approximately five hours a day, over five or six days a week. Once again, she strives to protect herself from exploitation brought on by herself alone and will endeavour to pace her psychic life, just as she does her more conventional existence.

QUESTION 29

Do psychics believe or know?

"A psychic is given impressions which help us to know. Without them we could not 'see.' Believing, on the other hand, is imparted by impressions and opinion of things, and it is something filtered by our life experiences and beliefs. During a session," Jessica affirms, "we must let go all those filters and exist only in the 'knowing energy' ever present with us and which emanates from… Spirit."

QUESTION 30

Is it true that a psychic because of intuitive abilities and knowledge, will have no fear of dying because of her knowledge, regarding the other side?

"This, I think, will depend on the psychic," Jessica offers. "Personally, I have no fear of dying because of what I have seen and know, but am I looking forward to death?

"Hell no!" she exclaims, "but it does not scare me. It is something I do not ponder or dwell on, but I choose instead to enjoy every minute of my life." One can readily believe this is one conviction Jessica freely advises everyone to do, because to her, "life is precious."

QUESTION 31

Is life for a psychic more tranquil, less stressful, and more meaningful, because of the 'gift?'

"At times, yes," Jessica declares, and explains further, "sometimes just knowing there is a Divine Purpose and Path instills peace, but other times these same insights can be stressful."

She shares just such an incident which involves her sixth sense and is an obvious burden to her. "Over the past month," she reveals, "I have been plagued with visions of planes crashing. These dreams are precognitive or clairvoyant, because the day after such a dream had invaded my sleep, a plane did crash and although I knew it would happen, I had no control over the outcome. This is beyond stressful and nerve-racking.

"After all, I cannot telephone the FAA to warn them, at least not without causing one heck of a stir, or being locked up in a psych ward somewhere diagnosis: 'crazy.' It is simply a situation I must accept and control to the best of my 'psychic' ability, but it is something not easily done."

QUESTION 32

Do clients ever become angry or frustrated with the information gleaned from your readings?

"If a person comes to me with lies, then yes, they may become miffed when I read and know they are being false. Often they cannot believe I know what I do or how I know. For example, there are times when I speak with clients who are incredibly devoted to a certain someone who does not return the affection.

When I mention this, the response is often one of frustration and anger on the client's part."

Another example, Jessica continues, "If I tell a client they are barking up the wrong tree when they offer love and affection to another who does not reciprocate, the reaction is often anger and disbelief. Frequently, clients seek validation of their feelings from Spirit through me, or they desire comfort and confirmation the object of their affection will eventually see the client for the wonderful person he or she is and fall madly in love.

"Believe me; it is difficult and sad when the message through me but from Spirit to a client, specifies a particular relationship is hopeless.

"I will strive to ease the hurt," Jessica concludes, "and I do cite positive encouragement which will hopefully motivate and instill excitement, but mostly will encourage my client to pursue a more suitable relationship. If a client engages me to placate or only tell them what they want to hear, I am quick to advise they have come to the wrong psychic."

QUESTION 33

Who are your clients by way of their backgrounds, professions, etc.?

People from every walk of life engage Jessica, who reveals, "I see everyone from teachers, doctors, lawyers, entertainers, homemakers, young folks and old, including other psychics, and I strive to be of help to each and every one, despite the reason or any skepticism they might bring to the reading."

QUESTION 34

Do you see, or have you seen a spirit, angel, or any such entity in your work?

"Every single day! I 'see' the dead and I 'see' Guides and Angels both objectively and subjectively. By this I mean, both literally and imminently. I can 'see' them with my two eyes but I can also 'see' each and every one of them with my mind's eye."

QUESTION 35

Given how hard you work in a day; do you have a fear of burning out?

"Sometimes," Jessica admits, "but my Guides are tough cookies just like me, and when they perceive a potential burnout is on my horizon, they will slow me down, so I can rest and reinvigorate." She adds, "I am more conscientious now about making sure to schedule in some 'ME' time every single day. If I don't, my burnout would have occurred a long time ago."

QUESTION 36

If you foresee illness or death will you discuss these revelations with a client? If not, what if your disclosure would encourage a client to seek medical help and then may become well? Or, what if you could change the course of an accident or injury to a person, would this embolden you to speak out?

"If I am shown an illness it is because I am meant to help the client find a path to wellness, so to help them, YES, I will speak up. If I am given an image of an impending accident but it is shown in such a way as to actually know WHO that person is and when the incident will occur, I will reveal especially if there is any probability whatever to alter it."

Jessica believes her Guides also show her events she cannot prevent and in these instances, she is forced and must subsequently resign herself to accept the inevitable. But in cases of disaster or other world dangers, her Guides will reveal these occurrences, so she can warn her clients to be circumspect and cautious in their travel arrangements. But when Spirit is forthcoming with information, Jessica is certain to reveal every detail, particularly if it may help the client prevent an incident. "On the other hand," Jessica concludes, "even if I don't 'see' illness, people will often question me as to when they might die, and yes, I am often asked this question, but I will not respond. I refuse to give anyone their expiration date upon request, because doing this would place gloom and doom over them for the rest of their lives. No one, but most especially a psychic has a right to do this. It is not my path, nor is it my purpose nor is it of any paranormal to convey such information.

"No way! No how," Jessica responds.

In this our final conversation respecting the book, she reveals details regarding her dear friend, Shauna, who passed away September 2014 following a severe illness. This was an extremely stressful time for Jessica because her paranormal insight had revealed months earlier her friend would soon pass. She could not, would not, did not, impart this knowledge to anyone including Shauna, but kept it inside and instead continued to visit her friend in an effort to cheer and comfort her.

When she was with Shauna there seemed to be a marked improvement in her condition for a time, but Jessica knew what was to come and inevitably it did. Once her friend passed, sad as it was, Jessica said she immediately felt lighter inside because she knew her friend had been released from pain. Following the memorial service, family and friends gathered to commemorate and honour Shauna and after visiting with them, Jessica went into the house to help tidy and clean up. There, she was instantly confronted by Shauna's father, who undoubtedly, because of the alcohol he had consumed, both rudely and aggressively verbally attacked her. He insinuated she was a charlatan and effectively accused her and the psychic community of being imposters. In this mood, he challenged Jessica to prove her paranormal ability by describing his mother, who was long deceased.

Generally, Jessica admits she ignores such criticism and effrontery, but because this vehemence was uttered in front of the other folks, who were present to honour Shauna's memory, she reacted tempestuously and perhaps irrationally. "Then and there I literally revealed details to him regarding his family. I disclosed his mother had died in childbirth when he was ten, related he was one of seven children and he had one sister who suffered with a mental illness. I added he and his sister were taken from their father at a young age because he had been incredibly abusive to his wife and finally, I revealed his mother's name was Madeline and also her surname, which for obvious reasons is omitted here."

The next day, serious and sober, Shauna's father apologized to Jessica and left both awed and chastened. He was now fully cognizant his accusations were misguided because Jessica had spoken true, and finally, he also admitted the paranormal world Jessica occupied was certainly credible. Jessica, who had attended the memorial partly because of respect for her friend also believed, she as a psychic, could provide counsel, comfort and enlightenment to the other mourners. In the case of the father she certainly did and Jessica admits the entire situation with Shauna's father had so extremely annoyed her; she had no regret whatsoever when she "took him on."

Shauna may have passed but her continued involvement in Jessica's life is striking to say the least. After her death, Jessica felt it was time to give her psychic/medium powers a rest, so she tried to downsize for a week, but for the most peculiar of reasons. "I knew Shauna would hang around, 'chatting away,' wanting to talk about this and that almost as if she were still present on Earth. Sure enough she was there and she was not only a presence in my life but she also invaded my son Joseph's life too." You see, Dear Reader, Jessica's son also is a psychic/medium and his young life is equally populated by Spirits from the spectral domain. Jessica claims, "These Spirit Guides have found 'friends' they trust here on earth and most assuredly, we are equally trusting of them."

ABOUT JOSEPH

YOUNG PSYCHIC
JOSEPH COSTELLO
FITCHBURG, MASSACHUSETTS

Imagine if you will a little boy still a toddler, who begins at this tender age, almost before he could speak, to exhibit paranormal abilities. Meet Joey Costello, born September 8, 2004, who is one such child, and one who would project thoughts and feelings to his mother by using gestures and looks, only she in the family, could understand. She too is psychic, so she was able to readily recognize her son was equally 'gifted,' which made them kindred souls in the paranormal sphere.

It was clearly evident and left no doubt when at age five, Joey chatted nonstop to his mother about a dog he knew. He vividly described the animal and revealed her name was Maisey. "This was all very well," his mother said, "but he had never seen this dog in his young life." Later she showed him photos of several dogs but revealed no details, when he suddenly selected a photo of a Sheltie dog his mom once had and said, this was the animal with whom he conversed. And yes, her name was Maisie. The little dog passed away two weeks before Joey was born and although the dog was never mentioned, Joey nonetheless, fully interacted with her, just as though she were alive.

It takes a psychic mother to even begin to comprehend how life will evolve for Joey as he grows older, but it is certain the 'gift' will undoubtedly continue to manifest in endless situations. "There is no sense in telling him he can't use it," his mother reveals, "because it can't be turned off. I do, however, advise him to keep some of his impressions to himself, especially around his sister if they happen to involve the departed. This is imperative, because such talk causes her to have vivid and frightening nightmares."

Meteorologists had nothing on Joey when he was still in kindergarten, because he could predict snow days well in advance of the events. These were among his first revelations and were often more accurate than those proclaimed by the television forecasters. It was common knowledge, even when he was the tender age of five, his family and friends counted on his predictions, because it was perfectly 'normal' for him to predict rain or snowfall in the community.

It will be necessary, however, as he grows up for his parents to encourage continued controlled use of his 'gift' in an attempt to ensure it is used cautiously and conservatively. "This is easier said than done," his mother admits, "because all we can do is talk to him about the appropriate ways to expend his psychic energy and hope he listens.

"We warn Joey it is unwise for him to communicate with each and every Spirit, who will hover around him or he will become inundated." Other advice from his parents pertains to impressions he may 'envision' which may relate specifically to someone he knows. "Should this occur," his mother adds, "we advise it is perfectly permissible, even advisable, to keep these visions to himself. It is obvious if people are unaware of Joey's 'gift' such revelations could be alarming and stressful."

Because of his young age, Joey's friends are not completely aware of his 'gift' and as it is with all boys around this age, his mother believes, "Their interests are different and can centre more around Legos and superheroes than anything paranormal. Thank goodness, because this will help to ensure the majority of his days will be completely typical and similar to that of any ten-year-old boy. I don't see this changing any time soon, but we will continue to caution him that it is more prudent to keep his impressions to himself, mostly because it is difficult for any child to be seen as different."

Regardless of their excellent intentions, however, she knows there is no doubt Joey is different and change will be unavoidable as the years go by. His 'gift' will gain prominence and become public knowledge, but even so, he is a fortunate young man because his parents understand his 'gift' and will try to ensure as he matures, his paranormal life will be restrained and manageable. If his parents have any influence and control, Joey's 'gift' will manifest itself slowly and carefully, but now at his young age, there is no one who can positively foretell the future, for this young and 'gifted' psychic.

What will be will be.

REFERENCES

PSYCHIC JESSICA
REFERENCE EDIE SCOTT
FITCHBURG, MASSACHUSETTS
U.S.A.

Although Edie Scott had visited various spirit mediums before she met Jessica, there is no doubt in her mind this psychic is the most gifted. Edie's continuing questions about her life, her family and her future were all factors which propelled her to find answers. In this quest, she had previously sought help from psychics, tarot readers, palm readers and the like, but she never seemed to completely connect with anyone.

Satisfaction eluded her until she found Jessica on 'Groupon,' which is an Arizona-based company that assists groups or individuals expand their companies or services. When Edie initially met with this psychic, she felt immediately at ease, as Jessica provided her with a brief background and explained her services.

"What Jessica discussed in our initial meeting was incredibly accurate, enlightening, and more than I had hoped for," Edie declares. "Since that first reading, my husband passed away, but before he died Jessica provided guidance as I planned his continuing care and even now, with ongoing and difficult family issues, I continue to consult with Jessica every six to eight weeks for advice."

"What astounds me but also provides genuine comfort, is through Jessica I am able to communicate with my husband and other deceased loved ones, who, from the other side, continue to provide help and guidance, in daily decisions I must make."

Edie is equally adamant in her belief Jessica has the ability to initiate specific paranormal conversations, and will frequently reveal information with incredible clarity, all of which Edie can and does validate and authenticate. She finds Jessica's gift so phenomenal she regularly refers beloved family members and friends to her and each one, she claims, has expressed complete astonishment and satisfaction with the psychic.

Edie concludes she is incredibly grateful to Jessica for sharing her gift, "Most specifically because her paranormal intervention continues to enhance and ease my existence." As if to substantiate this conviction, Edie has requested her children inform Jessica when she passes, "not for me," she declares, "but because Jessica will comfort them and knowing this, will ensure my tranquility when my time comes."

JESSICA COSTELLO
REFERENCE TARA RYAN
BOSTON, MASSACHUSETTS

Serious illness, not hers but that of the mother of Tara's best friend, who was morbidly ill, was the urgent and powerful impetus for her decision to seek Jessica Costello for psychic advice. "My friend's mother was afflicted with breast cancer complicated by multiple sclerosis, which meant finding immediate help was imperative for family members. Ultimately, they received superb advice and guidance from Jessica, as to how to provide the best of care during this dreadful experience.

"Although their mother passed away, the family has no doubt whatsoever the psychic's every word and wise counsel proved to be tremendously helpful and accurate during this grievous situation." Tara reveals Jessica provided meaningful comfort to her friend, but what was equally important is the fact she also conveyed messages from other family members who had passed. These messages proved to be accurate and equally helpful to Tara's friend as they endured her mother's traumatic illness. When Jessica refunded payment for a cancelled session because of prevailing serious events, Tara was dumbstruck. "What a difference from my previous experiences," she reflects, "but Jessica's patience and understanding throughout were astounding attributes."

Although Tara's experiences with other psychics before she met with Jessica were all disappointing, she felt an instant warm welcome in her communication with this psychic. "Too often in the past," she vents, "I felt I was being judged and strung along while the clock ticked and the offending psychics simply charged more for services rendered, or to be more realistic, for advice not provided."

She adds in no way, shape or form did Jessica make her feel insignificant, rather, she was sincere, confident without arrogance and Tara is still awestruck with Jessica's unparalleled instincts. "She imparted information above and beyond that of any other psychic, with whom I had consulted in the past."

Tara found Jessica on a website where for payment, a psychic can literally advertise individual services, but contends she was hesitant to make her initial contact, due to her lingering apprehension from previous readings with other mediums. "They were incredibly intense and awkward, and I didn't know what to expect with Jessica, but it was unnecessary to have been concerned," she exclaims. "Jessica exhibited a caring, considerate, truthful demeanour and one which conveyed how obviously committed she is to her clients." Tara notes her experiences with previous psychics who disappointed and dismayed her, may clearly illustrate to others how important it is when seeking psychic counsel to be circumspect and cautious. "Be diligent and do your homework," she advises.

Tara contends it was obvious moments into the session Jessica was there to help her. "From that first meeting, I was speaking with a friend and one who was genuinely interested in providing guidance and clarity to me. Important events in my life were about to occur and Jessica was there to serve my best interests. In other words, she did not simply tell me what I wanted to hear so I would return, but rather she told me the truth." She concludes Jessica has never been wrong about any of her romantic interests either, and laughingly admits the psychic is, "A much better navigator of my life than I am. To have personal counsel and insight from someone so incredibly 'gifted' and who honestly cares about me are priceless."

JESSICA COSTELLO
REFERENCE NANNETTE D'AGOSTINO
SAN TAN VALLEY, ARIZONA

Nannette D'Agostino was no stranger to psychic readings, most of them from referrals, but she was always unhappy with each one and claims they were consistently inaccurate and pricey. Then she discovered the website, 'Best American Psychics,' where she found Jessica Costello. "I was looking for reasonable pricing but authenticity was equally important, so the fact this site vetted their psychics as reliable and genuine, my confidence to find someone was bolstered."

Nannette was also looking for a psychic who could read from email and telephone contact, and despite the numerous available choices it was in truth, Jessica's photo that ultimately attracted her. "Her face, her smile, her sincerity seemed to shine through, so I arranged a reading and felt no apprehension right from the beginning."

"I was going through an awful time in my life and desperately needed someone who could provide an accurate synopsis of what was happening to me and why everything seemed to be out of control. Because earlier sessions with psychics had been through email, it was essential our connection must take place over the telephone." Nannette immediately found Jessica to be caring and genuinely interested in her situation and when they discussed the sense of loss which overwhelmed her when her mother and nephew passed away within six months of each other, Jessica and Nannette bonded with a rapport which endures to this day. "Jessica seemed to actually feel my anguish, almost as if she assimilated with my pain. She cut through the 'bull' and said my mom and nephew are happy and content on the other side, so why would I not be equally happy?"

She harbours no doubt through Jessica, she is able to converse with her loved ones and further, she believes the psychic imparts messages to her from them. "Through Jessica there is an absolute, positive and genuine connection with my family, which ensures my peace and serenity." Nannette is moved because the psychic readily responds to follow-up questions contained in notes she sends to Jessica, who "Stays current as to how life is unfolding for me."

"She even seems to connect with my dog, but equally important are the healing requests I seek for loved ones when needed. Jessica will immediately respond without question. I love speaking with her but not simply because she connects me to the other side, but because she also ensures my life is on track. Heck," she laughs, "Jessica's support is much better than seeing a psychiatrist." Although the loss of her mother was Nannette's catalyst to initially search for Jessica, there were other serious reasons she required intervention. "I made some important decisions," she admits "which did not work out. I was unemployed for more than a year after I relocated geographically to care for my mother, and there seemed to be nothing but negativity after negativity, as my life rapidly changed, but not for the better. I was lost and indecisive as insurmountable problems seem to affect my daily life."

Readings with Jessica provided the help Nannette required to 'get moving' and her advice was entirely accurate. The psychic said she would buy a home in January and she was to look for something 'blue.' Incredibly, she had seen a house she liked but felt it was too expensive. Jessica advised her to wait for the price to drop, which she did, but what was even more amazing to Nannette, was seeing the 'blue' fire pit in the backyard.

The psychic revealed both her guides were 'screaming' at her to ensure Nannette return to this house which she did and what next occurred was uncanny. Without prearrangement, two realtors unexpectedly appeared while she was there so "I mentioned my interest in this house. We talked as we toured and 'yep', I am now the owner, moved in, completely comfortable and secure." Following this development, Jessica soon mentioned a new job would materialize for me, so I began my search in earnest. She had sensed workplace difficulties where I was currently employed but then predicted a wonderful change was on its way. Nannette concludes with a glowing reference for Jessica. "I do not have sufficient adjectives to describe her. She is an absolute doll and I don't know where my life would be today without her guidance. Her 'gift' has navigated me through the absolute roughest year of my life and I mean the roughest, no exaggeration."

Jessica has sent Nannette crystals, sage and when she went off to the job interview, the psychic called but did not charge her for tips as to the required qualifications which were necessary for the advertised position. Additionally, she continued to advise Nannette during what turned out to be a successful search. "Who does this in the psychic business?" she asks, but then answers her own query, 'no one does.'

"Many operatives in this field charge exorbitant fees and offer very little, but also significant is to know Jessica never makes one feel she is in a hurry. I would love to meet her in person, give her the biggest hug and tell her, she is an awesome and 'gifted' human being, who is a blessing in my life."

A FINAL NOTE

Jessica Costello lives in Fitchburg, Massachusetts with her husband and her children, Samantha, age 6 and Joseph, age 10.

She maintains as 'normal' a family life possible, but considering she is constantly surrounded by Spirits, who manifest at will, all of the time, one wonders how she maintains her sanity. She is never alone because she is with her family, or because her Spirits are omnipresent.

This is her life and she loves it. Helping others if she can, by 'listening' to her Spirits, is her destiny, her purpose and it is one she takes as seriously as she does the issues and problems her clients bring to her. She does not differentiate a psychic session from a medium session because more often than not she simply rolls them in together. If a client requires life guidance and a Spirit is present and making himself known, Jessica's role is to be the conduit and convey the message. If she ignores it, the Spirit will hang around throughout the session or in the worst case scenario, stay around for a few days until she does.

Jessica chuckled when she related there were enough dead people around her on any given day to ensure she is careful she does nothing to annoy them, which could cause any one of them to hang around and bug her. She doesn't do house clearings, but if such a request is made, she will refer to one of two trusted, thorough, logical and ethical groups, who do this sort of thing. If they falter and need assistance, she has been known in the past, to go in and 'boot' the presence out.

This psychic has a suggestion for readers before her story is complete. "I think everyone should sage their home at every change of the season."

"Why? You might ask," for which she gives this explanation. "Basically, it is energetic cleaning which will clear stale energy and is comparable to the deep spring cleaning we do in our homes. Beware, however, because sage from the spice section does not work well, mostly because it is almost impossible to get it burning." She purchases her sage from an Arizona Health Food Store, http://www.nativesage.org/. because of the high quality at a reasonable price. Her blog regarding the correct methodology to cleanse can be found at http://psychicjessicac.com/smduging-101/if you have a mind to try it. Jessica has a singular way of describing her life, her work, her interests, her family and herself, to the point she is truly one of a kind. A few adjectives to aptly describe her might be intrepid, skillful, efficient, effective and confident. One fact seems assured, there can be no ghost or entity who will win any challenge with her. She won't have it, and she isn't one bit afraid to tell them to 'get lost.' If you wish to reach Jessica Costello, you will find her at:

    www.psychicjessicac.com
    Email: admin@PsychicJessica.com
    Telephone: 978.571.9880
    Her fees are:
    $65.00 for half hour psychic session
    $120.00 for full hour long private session

Be warned, however. She brooks no deceit and tolerates no nonsense, but you can be certain Jessica and her Spirits are on your side, if you are genuine and straightforward with them.

PSYCHIC

SHARON JOHNS
CHESTNUT MOUNTAIN
BRASELTON, GEORGIA
U.S.A.

AUTHOR'S NOTES

SHARON JOHNS
BRASELTON, GEORGIA
U.S.A.

There have been numerous occasions during the time I have been working on this book, when I have been asked to explain how the subjects who are featured herein were selected. Perhaps my relationship with Sharon Johns will help define more precisely than previously divulged how the five working psychics were chosen beginning with her. It was late in 2013 when the idea to write this narrative came to me, an account of which is covered earlier in this chronicle, but let it be said that although I had the thought to do it, the methodology and elaboration of the how and who, had yet to materialize.

How in the world I remember thinking, how in the world will I begin, because I know nothing about the subject and I certainly didn't have the acquaintance of one psychic, never mind four and then the five, to feature? It was obvious there was only one way to find them and that was to research, research and then research again, which I did over hours that eventually turned into months until finally I selected the first one, made initial contact before moving onto the next. Searching the web interminably, calling endless psychics over time, reviewing credentials and reputations, as much as is possible in this field, I finally contacted Sharon Johns, to enlist her in the project. It isn't a simple matter to cold call someone like her and then to quickly and succinctly explain not only who you are but what her role in the book will be. A sense of trust must be quickly established during that initial telephone call to be followed immediately by an email which will further define intent, the writer's personal and professional characteristics, but even more important, the role each individual psychic, including her, will have in the book.

This format had to be explained to each psychic with the singular purpose to entice that person to come aboard. I readily admit this strategy required all my persuasive skills, so you can imagine, Dear Reader, my relief and delight when something clicked between us and in good faith, Sharon agreed.

Correspondence followed, but unfortunately, the inevitable vicissitudes that percolate into a full life interfered, so it took considerable time all the way to November 2014, before I finally contacted Sharon again. Elation and exhilaration followed, when I learned her enthusiasm and willingness to be a part of the book, remained.

What struck me immediately about Sharon as her story unraveled was to learn of her profound trust in God, in heaven, and in angels, from whom she believes her healing powers originate.

It is from these sources which she claims are given to her through and from her faith that has allowed Sharon, for more than 35 years, to serve her clients not only as a psychic, but as a spiritual counsellor. This psychic is one who sincerely attributes her 'gift' to angels and guides, whom she believes are ever present and who actually dwell side by side with each one of us, and are ever ready to provide assistance if we would but ask.

Sharon believes it is her calling to help others but she can only successfully achieve this through the intervention of her heavenly sources. She claims they offer guidance, as she assists her clients to find love, peace and joy in this life and beyond even here one day, in heaven. This psychic contends God's love does not distinguish either time or space, because it is ever present and if one considers the testimonials she receives from clients the world over, who praise her message, then one has to believe Sharon has proven her spiritualism is tried and true, as she pursues her singular goal to provide assistance to those in need.

THE EVOLUTION OF PSYCHIC

SHARON JOHNS
BRASELTON, GEORGIA

QUESTION 1

Are you a psychic medium?

"I am a medium," Sharon affirms, "I see and hear, or to put it simply, I can contact the dead if they are willing to come forward. They have their jobs to do as I have mine, which means they cannot always be summoned." It is comparable to calling someone here on Earth but who is not at home, and subsequently, the telephone remains unanswered. Sharon acknowledges it is her experience that when a specter refuses to be summoned, a psychic can do nothing about it but wait and try again later.

QUESTION 2

Is there a difference between a psychic and a psychic medium? Please define each one.

"Yes, there is a difference," Sharon believes, and explains a psychic can look into the future to a degree and further, because they can often help others with problems and dilemmas. A medium, however, can journey further into the paranormal domain to contact those who have passed over.

QUESTION 3A

At what age did you discover you had this wonderful but supernatural 'gift?"

"When I was growing up," Sharon recalls, "it was never spoken of and frankly, I thought everyone could see the people I could see and I also believed it was simply natural to know the things I did." Sharon's realization she was different occurred when she was eleven years old and the event which illuminated her difference, is as strange to her today as it was then.

"Despite incredulity that one could have such an experience," she reveals, "I witnessed an apparition who appeared as would be any normal human being, until that is he walked through a wall. I did not imagine or hallucinate this," she emphasizes, "I saw what I saw." Sharon will divulge additional details about this astonishing episode, as her story continues.

QUESTION 3B

Did your mother or father know you were so gifted, and if so, did they ever advise you, when you were young, to keep this 'gift' to yourself?

Sharon honestly believes her mother and father not only didn't know when she was very young, but when they finally did, she is certain they didn't know what to do with her. It was easier to simply ignore the difference, she states, and amazingly, as it happens, Sharon also has two sisters who were then, equally extraordinary as children.

"When I had an experience as a child and told my parents, they would attempt an investigation but always after the fact, which meant there was nothing left to scrutinize." There was one time Sharon remembers when her sister, who also had the gift of paranormal vision, envisioned at age eleven their father being burned by a mechanic's torch. Later, when this event actually happened, it so frightened her, she literally closed down her 'gift' and never used it again. "My other sister," Sharon explains, would 'astral project' herself to exciting places and although her body was stationary, her spirit would allow her to roam anywhere she pleased. The negative side of this phenomenal ability, however, offered no guarantee as to where she would land or be where she wanted to be. So it was after such an experience she accepted the warning those astral trips could be dangerous. She finally shut down her paranormal power and chose instead to travel by more accepted methods.

QUESTION 4A

Apart from knowing you had the 'gift' what were you like as a child?

Sharon promptly admits as a youngster she was a recluse. "I was raised by my grandmother until I was eleven or twelve and I was extremely shy and quickly learned to be self-sufficient. I stayed pretty much to myself in school and because of this, I must have been aware even back then I was different from the other children."

QUESTION 4B

Was your childhood ever affected positively or negatively by the 'gift?'

"I didn't give it much thought when I was a kid," Sharon maintains, "although I remember having enormous empathy for others." She relates an early but strange memory when she was in first grade. "My granddad would drive me to school and it was a curious fact he would enter the driveway the wrong way, even though the proper entrance was almost traffic free.

"He was constantly told to drive back out and enter the proper way, but why he did this, I do not know. I was certainly aware it was unusually the source of some embarrassment for me because it ensured we were noticed, which was something I didn't want to be. I never could determine if he was simply being obstinate or whether he had some esoteric reason for this behaviour.

"Equally profound is a memory of a school principal who was supposed to be in the lunch room at noon to ensure students were adequately fed. "It was odd to see him there one day," she remembers, "because he seldom was. Instinctively, I knew it was because his supervisor was monitoring him, and even at that young age, I reckoned his concern was for himself not for the students." Even now Sharon believes these thoughts, followed by her cogent reasoning, were unusually advanced for a beginner in school, but she believes such deductions were revealed to her solely by way of her 'gift.'

"How many kids in grade school ponder such situations" she queries? "Very few," she replies.

QUESTION 4C

Did other children recognize you were different?

"Quite frankly," Sharon admits, "I wasn't around other kids too much, so for them to even observe my actions were different would have been difficult." In truth, Sharon also tried to mask her true persona and was never obvious about her 'gift.'

"I didn't want to stand out in any way," she recalls.

QUESTION 4D

What were your teen years like?

"My teen years were spent with my mother," Sharon says, and recalls it was during this time when she witnessed the wall incident mentioned earlier. She offers an explanation for this bizarre event.

"It is as real to me today as when it happened," she reveals. "That man walked out of the wall in the living room as my sister and I sat in front of a window fan trying to cool off. He simply appeared, passed between us and then disappeared, but I remember wondering at the time why he was in such a hurry.

"I believed then as I do now all these years later that this experience was for me, a glimpse into another dimension or place because this vision was as clear as day. The man wore sack clothing which fell to his knees, his feet were clad in sandals as described in the Bible, and amazingly, as he passed through, he kicked up dust which was astounding, and made me ponder where in the world the dust had come from." This memory remains profoundly astonishing for Sharon, who admits her sister, who was seated at her side did not see the phantom but Sharon said, "I did, and nothing has or ever will dissuade my memory."

QUESTION 5

How did the revelation that you possess this 'gift' make itself evident to you?

"I cannot remember a time when I did not have an immense desire or on second thought, an overwhelming need to know more about the paranormal." Sharon admits she had other experiences which seemed to manifest when she was thirteen or fourteen, but her first concrete indication of having unearthly powers, was the experience when the man walked through the wall.

QUESTION 6

What was your first experience in this field?

"It was early in my teen years," Sharon recalls, "when my mom heard about a young girl near my age, who was an evangelist and who would be preaching in the district. The odd thing about her, however, is it was said that as she preached, she would place her hand on the floor where her print would remain in red even after she removed her hand. To my family, it seemed to be a miracle and we were determined to see for ourselves if this was true."

Here Sharon's recollection is uncanny, because as she dressed for the outing to hear the young evangelist preach, and subsequently determine for herself if the hand print hypothesis was actually true, the following occurred. "As I was dressing, my room suddenly filled with something similar to smoke, although there was no odour. A man then appeared in a hooded garment similar to the attire a monk would wear, and although he seemed somewhat intimidating and scary, I was not afraid. Despite his unspoken objection conveyed through Spirit that I should stay home, I was equally adamant nothing would prevent me from attending that church meeting. "Amazingly," Sharon continues, "he glared at me for a few more minutes and then disappeared in a cloud of smoke never to be seen again." Although she related the incident to her mom and grandmother, by the time they investigated, nothing remained to review, not even the residual smell of smoke. "Nothing more was said about this incident," Sharon concedes, "but it provided additional proof for me that I was definitely different."

QUESTION 7

Do you envision things before, as, or after they happen, or all of the above? If you can give an example (s) of each that would be beneficial?

"Certainly when I was a child the wall incident was witnessed as it happened," Sharon recounts, "and as an adult I was always able to find lost items. As far as using my 'gift' to help others, I would say this didn't materialize to any degree until I moved to Florida. Here I found a spiritual church which offered lessons in the paranormal but were God and faith based. This was imperative for me, and it was here I learned to properly use my paranormal abilities, but always in conjunction with God and Christ as my guides."

It was also in this church where Sharon would in solemn prayer consistently reveal her desire to God to 'read' for others. If she could be of help to them, her 'gift' must be through and because of His intervention. She unequivocally believes when prayer comes from a sincere heart, God knows, and in His time will reveal His will. It was during this phase of her life when Sharon began to write her philosophy in a newsletter published by the church. Although she didn't understand why indecision and writer's block would at times impair her efforts, she kept trying. "I would compose, tear up and try again, until suddenly without warning, a word or an idea would come to me one at a time. I would see or hear a word, note them and then continue to write." Her work, published in church articles has been read by people in the United States, Canada, Brazil, South Africa, and England, but as far as she is concerned, this work only materialized because of divine intervention.

Sharon reveals she does see things before they happen, although she will at times implore her Sources to cease showing her negative revelations that she can neither change nor stop. She discloses one such incident where her psychic insight, still functional despite her plea to Source to give her some respite, was ignored. The incident involved her daughter-in-law, who was employed with a large company. She wanted and had worked incredibly hard to achieve a certain promotion but there were obstacles which could prevent her ultimate success. There was another applicant vying for the job, who would shamelessly lobby the boss, and cared not who knew it. "I had a vision of a strong blast of wind which would suddenly invade that office and sweep a number of people away. Coincidentally, there was another employee in the office, also a psychic, who visualized the same damaging wind, but neither she nor Sharon were able to determine precisely when this would occur. It would happen, but she admits, "it is a 'wait-and-see' foretelling." As it happened, Sharon's daughter-in-law did receive her well-earned promotion; the other applicant left the company exactly as Sharon had predicted, but it can be said, everyone in the company is still on watch for the gale yet to come.

QUESTION 8

Have you ever been incorrect in your readings?

"Not that I am aware, nor have I ever been told," Sharon declares, "and if I had to rate myself I would say I am 95 percent correct in my readings, but remember, I alone do not render the insight or the information in sessions. I ensure my clients know nothing predicted is written in stone, and often, despite advice or revelations in a reading, people will disregard my advice and go their own way. Such is human nature," she admits, "but frequently, I also receive feedback from numerous clients, who confirm the accuracy of my readings."

QUESTION 9

What, if any, was your worst, most scary or negative experience when using your 'gift?'

"I am never scared," Sharon declares, "because I am protected. However, once I was giving a reading, well, actually, it was more transchanneling, which is something I no longer do; it became clear there was a ghost close by. This apparition, although deceased, seemed to require help to cross over and when such a plight is revealed, I can and do help a soul to depart. I am never frightened when apparitions appear and although I have had endless experiences with hauntings I do not fear them. I know my goal is attained through God or helper angels, all of whom are ever present to protect and assist me."

During that transchanneling episode, however, Sharon discovered her client was teaching witchcraft and spells which was confirmed when a cryptic, acrid smell permeated the area. A voice from beyond asked if either she or the client had detected an odour, which in turn alerted Sharon there was evil afoot. She demanded the malevolent Spirit leave which it did. Sharon reveals although such appearances are unusual, they are also relatively common and normal. She also relates another negative event that occurred at an outdoor festival she had attended with a lady friend. As they walked, her friend became frightened and told Sharon she could see in the distance, her deceased mother approaching them. The friend also confided she had never liked her mother, nor did many other people. "She was deeply affected," Sharon remembers, "as we witnessed a cloud of grey mist begin to encircle the approaching woman. It seemed to rise upward from the ground to quickly form a complete circle around her.

"In that orbit I could see the faces of several more demons or 'lowers' as I call them, and it was only by calling on my paranormal powers was I able to order them to stop, to come no closer and leave, which they did, but it was a disconcerting experience, especially for my friend."

QUESTION 10

Do you have a favourite or most memorable client-based session?

She does not hesitate to reveal she has many favourite sessions and each one is singular and meaningful, but Sharon describes her psychic intervention into the 1988 Anita Lukander murder case in Florida, for which Former Navy Airman Peter Johnstone was convicted, remains the most traumatic and meaningful of all. Jailed for 14 months, awaiting the death penalty for a crime he did not commit, Sharon explains Johnstone was charged with the crime of murder and the mutilation of his fellow helicopter Navy airman, Anita Lukander.

Her involvement with this case began when the Office of the Public Defender decided after his conviction, that Johnstone might not be guilty, however, evidence to prove their strong belief was lacking. The United States Navy Cold Case Squad reopened the case and the Office of the Public Defender then brought Sharon into the investigation. Given no information, she recalls 'seeing' immediately Johnstone was innocent and shocked the lawyers when she predicted he would be free by March of that year. "Psychically, I recognized the deceased lady had died of strangulation and not from the inflicted stab wounds and further, her abductor had held her for two or three days before she succumbed. This poor victim had not been killed immediately as had been previously believed, but what was more revealing," Sharon states, was when "I 'visualized' a ring that was on the murderer's finger."

This ring became critical in the case when a composite drawing as described by the owner of the shop where it was pawned. It was also here where the police found guns stolen during the robbery, but in the drawing there was a ring on the killer's finger identical to the ring Sharon had envisioned and had earlier described to the public defender attorney.

She immediately implored the public defender to have private investigators pursue the leads she had so clearly revealed, but admits it took endless hours to search and find that particular drawing, from the many stored in the numerous case file boxes. Sharon, however, was assured the ring would be found and it was.

She recalls the second Johnstone trial continued for two weeks, but was made more difficult because the composite sketch was initially deemed inadmissible. During jury deliberations, one member believed Johnstone to be guilty but because it was an eleven to one vote for acquittal, the judge finally allowed the composite sketch to be shown to the jury. Reasonable doubt was ultimately established and the unanimous 'not guilty' verdict was rendered.

In March, just as Sharon predicted, Johnstone was exonerated and set free. Not only can this psychic take considerable satisfaction in knowing she was instrumental in gaining release for Johnstone, who was innocent but this event also opened professional doors she could not have imagined. A television program called, Psychic Detectives, selected her from within the 100,000-member paranormal community, to be featured on the program.

Her involvement with the Johnstone situation generated such an intense investigation it was decided to feature it in a special production. It seemed when one door opened for Sharon, another opportunity quickly surfaced, because soon after this, she was approached by a Japanese television program to appear over a two-year period in a program produced in Japan. "It didn't take long for me to accept the invitation," she admits, "because I love to travel, see new places, and I believe God was guiding me on this exceptional journey.

He wants me to enjoy my life and to appropriately use the 'gift' he has given to me." Her favourite session recollection doesn't end with the Johnstone story, however, because she immediately relates another psychic session that involved a comatose, injured soldier. After watching a program on television which featured Sharon, a lady from Canada called, to enquire if she would intervene in a case that involved her cousin.

The Canadian lady explained her cousin, a soldier, while deployed in Afghanistan, was severely injured in a suicide bombing and had suffered a severe brain injury. The doctors maintained he would never recover and advised the family to remove the life support system that kept him alive. Desperate and reluctant to follow this advice, the cousin implored Sharon to intervene but it is clear her decision to help was difficult. Despite using her 'gift' many times in the past, she admits never having intervened with anyone in a comatose state, but nonetheless, despite distance and the use of a telephone, she agreed to try.

"While on the telephone with the lady," Sharon recounts, "I tuned into this young man's Spirit, who immediately advised psychically he was still undergoing a process to either let go or stay. The Spirit then implored Sharon to tell his family he needed time to decide."

Their psychic conversations continued when next the young man said he was to be kept alive while he reviewed his choices, but told Sharon he didn't want to stay on earth as a vegetable. He beseeched her to tell his family 'not to worry,' and then incredulously indicated he was not in pain because he was not in his physical body. "I am with my family even when they are at home and I can see what they are doing."

Initially, the family disbelieved what they were told, until Sharon revealed to a visiting cousin the young man was profoundly agitated because he did not have a certain round metal object with him. At this point his cousin injected, "It is his medal he wants. He always keeps it with him." Once it was by his side again, he settled down and it was then the cousin revealed this incident to his mother, and revealed Sharon's involvement with her son.

The psychic told his mother her son constantly referred to nearby red gerber daisies, but his mother noted there were only yellow flowers in his room. Later, as she walked past the nursing station she saw red gerber daisies on the counter and was befuddled until Sharon explained her son's Spirit had seen them as he roamed the unit. This revelation brought immediate comfort to his family because to them, it was incredibly factual and realistic. A few days passed before Sharon received a psychic message from the young man. She was to inform his family he would awaken in seven to nine days, and as can be imagined their incredulity and that of the medical team was one of disbelief, but made credible because on the ninth day he did awaken. Soon he was walking with assistance, fully able to communicate, and only slight time passed before he regained all functionality other than his complete memory.

Today, certain memories have been restored, although he recalls nothing of the bombing and has no recollection of his communication with Sharon, whose reward comes by way of his resumption of a 'normal' life, which is described by his family, as Sharon's miracle.

The local television station in Atlanta, Georgia featured this case on an evening newscast, and when the anchor of that program was questioned as to why the story wasn't featured nationally because it had all the components of a 'great television movie' he offered no opinion. For him, their local coverage was sufficient and for Sharon it simply did not matter. Her reward occurred when the soldier began to live his life again.

QUESTION 11

How do you acquire your clients?

"Certainly through word of mouth and my website but it is also true many people became aware of me and then made contact following my appearances on various television programs. Such exposure is invaluable," she maintains, "but reputation is most important of all when it comes to clientele."

QUESTION 12

Can you, as a psychic manipulate a person for whom you are doing a reading?

"Emphatically no! Clients ask the questions but it is the Guides who provide the answers, although initially, I must also ensure a client is aware the more direct the question they ask, the more direct the answer will be."

Sharon confides she can see and hear the replies, but nothing is achieved or done without prior prayer, which raises her to a higher level. "Only then can I receive accurate and factual information for my client," she affirms.

QUESTION 13

Is there ever a time or with a certain kind of person where your 'gift' does not work, and, if so, why would this be?

"Honestly, never," Sharon contends. "Certainly there are skeptical clients who do not hide the fact they are, but the truth is after they ask their questions, it is obvious they clearly understand the relevancy of the answers." She refers to the many calls she receives from those same doubting clients, who will later confirm the information revealed did come true. "This makes me tremendously happy," Sharon concludes, "because it confirms I am doing my job."

QUESTION 14

Do you control your psychic power or does it have authority over you?

This is an issue which doesn't surface with Sharon because she contends she keeps her 'gift' blocked and does not tune in until she has specific questions that need answers. "Rarely do I get a brief glimpse of anything unless I summon information, so the ultimate authority remains with me."

QUESTION 15

Do you consider your psychic power a 'gift' or a 'curse?'

Emphatically and without hesitation, Sharon replies, "This ability is a direct and blessed 'gift' from God! I do this work to help others and I am truly blessed in so many ways because I can see, feel and know. But without God, I can do nothing."

Sharon relates an uncanny story about a recent experience when a gentleman from the 'other side' strolled through her hallway. She stopped him to say, "I bet you think I can't see you, but I do," and she reveals this is an apparition she has encountered several times since then. "He wears khaki attire similar to that in a recent advertising commercial. He is tall and exudes a gentle demeanour and freely communes with my pets, as he passes through my home. He means no harm and does not linger, but simply continues on his way to his destination, wherever that might be."

QUESTION 16

Do you have to summon your 'gift' or does it have a will of its own?

"No need to summon," Sharon affirms, "because God knows when I am going to read and in my prayers before a session, I implore for His help and any information I receive will be accurate and factual, because it does come from Him."

Sharon senses the replies to questions she is asked, and if she encounters lost ghosts around her, she can see them, hear them, feel them, and perceive their emotions. She will converse with them and if asked, will help them to pass over by engaging in earnest prayer. "It is only through prayer that I am able to function at a high and safe level," she declares.

QUESTION 17

How do strangers react to you when you encounter them? Do they have any idea or realization that you have the 'gift?'

"No one really knows," Sharon maintains, "unless they have seen me on television or been told about me. I teach art locally and even here, most people don't have a clue I have this 'gift,' but then again," she emphasizes, "I do keep it to myself."

QUESTION 18

Once people are aware you are gifted or have psychic powers, do they react with:
Skepticism?
Fear?
Disbelief?

Sharon ponders this question carefully before she discloses she is incredibly discreet before revealing to anyone who she is and what she does. She feels most people are open and respectful of her 'gift' and believes most everyone with whom she shares her calling, already know the kind of person she is and are open, receptive and without fear when in her company. Skepticism, fear and disbelief seem not to enter into her professional psychic life, because Sharon is who she is and her sincerity, concern and dedication to her clients obviously effaces any doubt. "My clients seem to completely believe in me, no matter what my message."

QUESTION 19

Do your psychic powers ever get you into trouble?

"Emphatically no," Sharon says, "because when something is not my business, or I am not invited to participate, I do not invade a person's private, personal space. An honourable psychic will never do this. You use this 'gift' only when your services are engaged, or when you have a client who seeks help through psychic intervention." Sharon is adamant she is extremely careful and private as she goes about her work and will not go where she should not be.

QUESTION 20

Do doors that would normally be difficult to enter, open for you because of your psychic powers?

"Yes! But only because God has a way of putting me where He wants me to be." Sharon relates an incident which occurred before she was approached to appear on a television program. This was an experience she desperately wanted, so as she walked through her home, she 'spoke' to God and said, "God, you have given me a gift and if you want me to use it you had better get busy, because I need your intervention."

Sharon believes people should converse with God and Christ, precisely as we do with anyone else. This is something she does and firmly believes prayer is heard when offered with heartfelt honesty. Two weeks after her fervent petition to God, Sharon received a call from a television program, followed by contact with another producer and soon after, not once but twice; there was contact from a Japanese television firm, all of which for her validates the power of prayer.

QUESTION 21

Are you a healer, and what is your definition of a healer?

"I do healing sessions on occasion but rarely," Sharon admits, "however, I will frequently pray for my clients and I do maintain a relationship with an exemplary healer in this medium, who is profoundly able to help those in need." Her friend, John Bueche, is a true healer and one who has Sharon's admiration and respect. "I lament he hasn't yet been able to fully convey his 'gift' to those who might need him, but then again he may not be quite ready. I am certain as he continues to assist me, he will continue to learn and develop his skills."

Sharon reluctantly reveals there are many psychically 'gifted' people, who must work at regular jobs for daily support. "This limits the time and effort needed to develop a clientele and consequently, this also means many ethically and evolving psychics are hindered in their objective to function day to day in this profession."

QUESTION 22

How do you control your 'gift' or does it need to be controlled?

"It doesn't require control," Sharon conveys, "I simply turn it off when I am not involved in a reading. It is impossible to be 'open' all the time, because of continuing interference and confusion in my surrounding environment. To be engaged in the psychic domain, it is necessary to stay tuned but it is equally important to know when to shut down." She reveals her son, also a psychic, cannot function if he remains constantly 'open' to the paranormal realm. "A psychic must stay grounded and embrace the quiet times and rest."

QUESTION 23

Is psychic power the same as intuitive power?

To Sharon they are the same and are similarly and simultaneously used in her profession.

QUESTION 24

Can the 'gift' be misused?

"Yes!" Sharon replies, and she regrets there are psychics with the ability to help others, but instead use their 'gift' to extort funds from clients." Although she will not divulge names, she refers to a client of hers who had paid a vast sum to another for psychic services, only to be deceived. Sharon later 'read' for this same lady, which ultimately produced excellent results. However, she still laments, it is deplorable this client and many others are abused by unsavoury psychics. "It is sad but true when this occurs," Sharon concedes, "but I believe these charlatans will eventually get back what they give and you can be sure, I do not and will never walk in their shoes."

QUESTION 25

Is it possible for one with the 'gift' to become arrogant in having it?

"Oh yes," Sharon replies. "This profession is similar to others in that ego can supplant purpose, but these psychics as a rule, don't practice very long. They are soon found out and I believe only God and our own selves, ultimately know what is truly in our hearts and what will be our intentions."

QUESTION 26

Because you believe your 'gift' comes from God, can it be purloined by the devil or evil forces?

"Oh yes," Sharon responds, "which is why prayer is so important. Only God knows one's heart and if a psychic's purpose is to help people, then He is there to provide." Sharon believes caution is imperative because evil forces or 'lowers' can intervene and ostensibly give the impression they are there to help. She recalls a friend who practiced spells with her 'gift' knowing full well she was being aided by the 'dark.' Trouble and remorse followed her practice, until finally she repented and since then has worked in the 'light' after a lesson well learned.

QUESTION 27

Fanciful as this question is, what is heaven like as envisioned by a psychic?

"This is a WOW question," Sharon exclaims, as she contemplates her reply. "There are days here on earth, although they may be few and far between, when life is akin to heaven. I have only to think of the beauties of nature, see my horse grazing in an open field of green, or feel a gentle breeze that cools the day and it is then these illustrations are for me, heaven on Earth."

Sharon believes we will see our loved ones who have passed when we reach heaven, and this place will be for each one of us, whatever we want it to be. She is equally certain that Jesus and His helpers are with us every day, whether we are here on earth or have passed over. For this psychic, it all comes down to her faith.

QUESTION 28

How many hours per week do you use your paranormal powers?

"Every day," Sharon avows, because messages will come to her regularly from her 'Guides' who want her to experience or be aware of something. "I will hear the voice of my Guide or I will feel the touch of an Angel, who reveal information but only in their own time. However," she admits, "I must also tune in to prepare myself before a reading."

QUESTION 29

Does a psychic believe or know?

"It takes both to succeed," Sharon asserts. "One must know you have the 'gift' but you must also accept you have it, if it is to be used."

QUESTION 30

Is it true that a psychic, because of her intuitive abilities and knowledge, would have no fear of dying because of her knowledge regarding the other side?

"For me there is no fear," Sharon declares. "Why would one fear when one absolutely knows? I certainly have no desire to immediately leave this world because I would like to see my grandkids grow up and perhaps even become a great-grandmother, but I also accept that God knows what is best for me, and happily, without question, I accede to His will."

QUESTION 31

If life for a psychic more tranquil, less stressful, and more meaningful, because of the 'gift?'

"Unfortunately no, not for me," Sharon admits, "because I still struggle with being a human here on Earth and like everyone else, I must endure the trials and tribulations of survival. I am blessed, however, to have peace in my soul and if I can acknowledge the presence of difficulties then let them go, everything will work out rather well. I try to remember the edict 'ask and thou shalt receive' and although this may sound incredibly religious, I do believe. Knowing and having faith in my source and trusting in that source sustains me." Sharon reveals she does not attend church services, where she feels strife and politics are much too prevalent and where peace eludes her.

'To each his own,' is her mantra; however, she is careful, she emphasizes, "That I do not impose my beliefs on anyone else. If organized religion aids one to cope then I say go for it, but as for me, I cannot and do not subscribe to conformist doctrines, especially those which advocate a life must be one way or another. My God is too omnipotent to be put into a box."

QUESTION 32

Do clients ever become angry or frustrated with the information gleaned from your readings?

"They don't seem to," Sharon declares, "rather they will often tell me how happy and enlightened their readings are, and many express a sense of peacefulness after the session ends." There is no doubt for Sharon these feelings evolve through her to her clients from the Source and the Light, who use her 'gift' to enlighten.

QUESTION 33

Who are your clients by way of their background, professions, etc.?

Sharon's clients come from many sources, from many professions and from every ethnic and spiritual background. "All those who come," she maintains, "seek guidance, help and hope, which is exactly what I strive to provide to each and every client."

QUESTION 34

Do you see, or have you seen a Spirit, an Angel, or any such entity in your work?

"As described previously in the description of the male spirit encountered in my home, I admit I frequently see Spirits and in fact, it is more the norm than the unusual for me to encounter entities from beyond. It would faze me much more," she declares, "if I didn't see them more than it does when they visit me."

QUESTION 35

Given how hard you work in a day, do you have a fear of burning out?

Sharon claims she has no fearing of overextending because she paces herself and ensures she has down time, not so much to manage the readings but rather to rejuvenate her body. She also relies on her Spirits and Guides to forewarn her, if she is about to overextend herself.

QUESTION 36

If you foresee illness or death will you discuss these revelations with a client? If not, what if your disclosure would encourage a client to seek medical help and then may become well? Or, what if you could change the course of an accident or injury to a person, would this embolden you to speak out?

Sharon explains for her to 'envision' something for a client, it is the client who must request the information. For example, if information comes to her in a reading which suggests a client should have a body scan, she will disclose this immediately, and if she is given a revelation which specifically concerns her client, she will also quickly share this information. "But in truth," she concludes, "I can only give to my clients what I receive from my Guides, whatever the information might be. That is after all why they consult with me."

REFERENCES

PSYCHIC SHARON JOHNS
REFERENCE MIMI O'HANNON
AMELIA ISLAND, FLORIDA
U.S.A.

One could deduce the first meeting between Mimi O'Hannon and Sharon Johns didn't go all that well. After a time Sharon was frustrated and Mimi was confused, because despite the psychic's continuous revelations, nothing made sense to her client. "It was 1996," Mimi recalls, "when I initially met with Sharon, and throughout our first session, she repeatedly told me there was a man, who had been in her presence the entire day and was waiting to speak with me. He kept giving her visual signs of a Kewpie Doll, Betty Boop and a young girl, about twelve years old, who was pushing a baby, in a black carriage called prams, long ago.

"Sharon kept asking what the symbols meant to me, but I had no idea about them or who the man was, while all the time she kept repeating, 'well, he is here and he keeps showing me these items.' I kept repeating, 'I don't know who he is,' until finally, in exasperation, we quit trying." Once Mimi arrived home, she immediately told her mother about the strange circumstances of the reading (her mother knew Sharon) and how this man had been trying to get her attention all day long. "We discussed the fact that Sharon will seldom get her 'feathers ruffled' but she was visibly frustrated, because I could not make the connection with this man from the other side." Within seconds, her mother looked at her with a blank stare and then burst out, "He is my father! He had a Betty Boop tattoo on his forearm, which looked more like a baby doll. The carriage is undoubtedly the one I used when I would take my sister, Marie, for a walk in the park." Mimi learned her mother and Marie were born ten years apart, so it was customary for her mom to take her sister for an outing, as was often decreed by her parents. "Mother was so incredibly excited we actually called Sharon again that very night, which resulted in an impromptu reading for mom. Sharon imparted message after message from her father, but I was simply astonished as to how tenacious both Sharon and my grandfather were, to bring about this connection."

In referencing the psychic, Mimi refers to the criminal case Sharon worked on at the Office of the Public Defender in Jacksonville, Florida. It was the State of Florida V. Peter Johnstone, the details of which are outlined in Sharon's story, and which were eventually featured in two television programs. "I keep compact discs of the second production because the entire case was incredibly extraordinary." When Mimi discusses Sharon's persona, she promptly refers to her profoundly caring attitude toward people in general. "She will readily read people without charge, including me and never declines to help, when her ability is required for a missing person's case, or if someone is in need regarding health issues, or may be worried about the well-being of a loved one. She has performed numerous 'body scans' for people and has the ability to 'see' a person internally. Subsequently, she will reveal their physical problems and I have witnessed occasions, when she will literally write down a diagnosis she cannot name or spell."

Although Sharon quickly affirms her 'gift to predict' originates with her Guides, who render the information she discloses, Mimi claims there are instances when these disclosures have worked out extremely well for her clients. "They will take the name and the revelations Sharon gives them to their doctors and often, those same physicians will immediately begin an exploratory diagnosis based on Sharon's visions. It goes without saying that Sharon is astoundingly accurate in her readings." Mimi contends she has personally witnessed Sharon identify a mass or a tumor for a client right down to its actual appearance. She once told Judy, who is an attorney with whom Mimi works that she was not to worry about a lump found in her breast because it was benign. "It was amazing when Sharon described the size, the shape and the colours in the mass. I then witnessed the doctors quickly arrange a lumpectomy and advised Judy they would also perform a mastectomy while she was anesthetized. The operation proceeded, the tumor was precisely as Sharon had described and later that same afternoon, we celebrated the good news at a bar called Hulihans, and yes, a healthy Judy was there too, proving once again how precise Sharon is in her readings."

For Mimi, it is difficult to explain how Sharon interacts with her clients. "You almost have to meet her to fully understand her energy because her appearance belies her ability. This petite, southern lady with short red hair and whose looks remind Mimi of Shirley MacLaine is composed and yet, she emits tremendous warmth to all. People tell me when they hug Sharon; they can actually feel her energy and this declaration is also expressed by even those, who are initially skeptical regarding her 'gift.' Because Sharon's readings are incredibly accurate, for more than 25 years Mimi has, without hesitation, introduced many of her friends to the psychic for readings. "I have placed my professional reputation on the line by using and recommending her, but this verifies how deeply I believe in her. I make no serious decisions in my life without obtaining Sharon's advice, and admit there are times when I will contact her about small concerns which hover in the bigger picture but trouble me. Her guidance, amplified by her guides, provides me a sense of comfort to know all is well."

Although Sharon and Mimi are personal friends, it does not trouble the client to share personal information with the psychic. "She is and has always been such a great friend, and friend to me means trust. Sharon is incredibly faithful, both personally and professionally, because with each other we are both open books, and this is something that will never change."

PSYCHIC SHARON JOHNS REFERENCE REBECCA MUELLER TALLAHASSEE, FLORIDA U.S.A.

Tragedy brought them together, but it is understanding and compassion that forms the basis of a relationship which has endured and grown since October 1993. After learning about her from a friend, Rebecca Mueller sought urgent guidance and consolation from psychic, Sharon Johns, in her desperation for help, comfort and knowledge, regarding a tragedy in her life.

"My sister was killed in a tragic car accident in November of 1992. The driver was the brother of her sister's best friend who survived, although he had been drinking. The first year following this horrifying event was a nightmare," Rebecca admits. "It seemed I was in a bad dream and my sister would soon return, but instead a deep depression consumed me for over a year, until I finally decided to seek help from Sharon."

The psychic, as a rule, will only read for a client in person, so for the first and only time in her life, Rebecca missed her college classes when she travelled by car to Jacksonville, Florida to keep her appointment with Sharon. That meeting and the resulting readings transformed her life, because Sharon was able to channel her sister. "This event changed my life forever because it fostered in me, a renewed sense of purpose and understanding. Sharon described the details of a bracelet my mom had received from her sister's best friend and only my mother and I understood the significance of this bracelet. It concealed a photograph of my sister, Suzie and her best friend, and it was the last picture ever taken of them. This revelation was overwhelming because it confirmed Sharon had channeled my sister and as a sense of indescribable peace descended, it was then I finally believed my sister was in that glorious place called heaven."

As Sharon continued her counsel with Rebecca, a sense of serenity, hope and faith descended as she literally and finally, accepted that life does continue after death. Although raised in the Catholic faith with an acceptance there is God and heaven, comfort and acceptance continued to remain elusive for her until she met Sharon. Her guidance restored Rebecca's faith. "Because my sister's death finally evolved into a deep spiritual experience, she opened my heart and mind, to finally accept I must continue to live my life, despite the pain and sense of loss. I must also strive to appreciate my sister's life and although I could miss her and grieve, I must also focus on the triumph of her life and not the tragedy of her death." Rebecca unequivocally believes Sharon's intervention provided her the impetus to accept the loss of her beloved sister, but it also bolstered her to believe she had special gifts of wisdom and insight, which had to be used and shared as she lived her life. "Since then, I continue to receive 'special knowledge' from her and I have learned to trust my instincts.

"Sharon has 'angelic' ways and exceptional 'gifts' along with an uncanny ability to channel those who have passed, which includes those who are gone but may be lingering in their own debate, as to whether they want to cross over. She does console but she will also remind clients despite adversity we must forge ahead. Where my life would be without her guidance is dubious, but today despair transforms to hope and comfort, along with a sense of direction to live each day joyously and completely.

"Since our first meeting, Sharon has become my second mother, who offers me guidance to cope with life's ups and downs. Her sweet demeanour whether she telephones or I see her in person is ever present as she encourages me to make sound decisions and smart choices. She cares about everyone and will break through pain and suffering to bring beauty and kindness to all." From their first meeting, Rebecca believes when Sharon speaks, it is as though her words are coming from her Guides or a higher power. The psychic believes this power is God himself, who through her, will continue to shine His white light into her readings. "Her primary purpose is to help others in their search for a sense of lightness, brightness and serenity in their lives."

When first they met, Sharon revealed to Rebecca there would be two out-of-state moves before she settled closer to her hometown, made true when in 1996 she moved to Charlotte, North Carolina and again in 1999, when she moved to Charleston, South Carolina. Sharon also predicted Rebecca would meet someone in 1996, who would request she move to another state and this also occurred.

Although it is personal and difficult to admit, Rebecca contends she recently ended a difficult relationship which was a source of anguish. "Out of the blue, Sharon, using higher powers through her Guides, called me to describe the details of this relationship and why it must end." Throughout the years, Rebecca has kept a written record of her conversations with Sharon, which she treasures and frequently reviews. "Each and every time, I am newly empowered to embrace change whenever it may come." Rebecca's entire life history is an open book to Sharon, who knows where she has been and where she is going and in this personal relationship, there is for both, a deep sense of comfort. "I share my deepest and darkest secrets and because we have both experienced trials and tribulations in this life, we are bound together in mutual understanding and compassion. Sharon will often refer to what she calls my special gift because I am non judgemental and keep an open mind when people share their troubles with me.

"Following my sister's death, Sharon restored my life and she did this again in 1998, when she brought comfort to me as she channeled my beloved grandfather, who had recently passed. For me, it confirmed my family is together in the Spirit world, where we will all reunite when life on Earth is done. Knowing this helps to make me be a better person and more able to live each day fully. I know I can do this until our family is together again on the other side."

Rebecca is confident Sharon will continue to guide her regardless of the time of day or the celebration of the year. "She will be there throughout any crisis, because she is a kind and endearing presence, who is dedicated to help me be a better person. Knowing her is a gift from heaven and I am blessed she is helping me to live my life in trust and faith."

PSYCHIC SHARON
REFERENCE JERRYE D. LAIL
LOGANVILLE, GEORGIA
U.S.A.

During what is nearly a lifetime of friendship between Jerrye Lail and Sharon Johns, there is a certain incident for Jerrye which clearly demonstrates Sharon's psychic prowess. It occurred when a co-worker of hers was experiencing a difficult time and sought psychic guidance and subsequently asked Jerrye if she could arrange a session with Sharon.

Because Jerrye believed Sharon could help her colleague, she quickly arranged a meeting in her home but told Sharon nothing about her friend, other than the fact they worked together. "When Sharon arrived, she asked my friend's name, wrote it on a legal pad, and then quickly declared she wanted no further information. I did not stay for the reading," Jerrye recalls, "but I did remain long enough to witness Sharon furiously writing down information that was apparently coming to her from her Guides." When the session ended, Jerrye recalls, nothing was discussed among the three ladies until the next day at work when her friend confided shock and amazement as to how many 'secrets' Sharon knew about her. She was flabbergasted when the psychic described her childhood right down to a doll she had back then. She also described the relationship the co-worker had shared with her mother, and included details, as to how her mother had passed away.

"My friend was mystified and astounded, but declared Sharon was completely accurate in her every revelation, but what truly astonished her was the psychic's revelation my coworker would divorce and remarry in the future, which eventually occurred precisely as Sharon had predicted."

Jerrye describes Sharon as a caring and dedicated psychic and one who will volunteer to help law enforcement with cold cases, yet never seeks a fee once the crime is resolved. The psychic will also read for people who cannot afford to pay but still require guidance in their lives. She further reveals many months will pass when suddenly out of the blue, a client whose life Sharon improved, will forward unsolicited payment, long after the reading was done. When it comes to the actual reading, Jerrye discloses Sharon will do everything possible to ensure her client is comfortable and relaxed, settled into a comfortable chair with water or a snack if needed, and then encouraged to be completely relaxed. Once a calm, tranquil atmosphere prevails, Sharon quietly and gently begins by ensuring her clients any information she imparts will be accurate and true, because her 'gift' comes from God.

Jerrye admits because she and Sharon have been friends for so long, it is impossible for her to receive a reading from the psychic. "We are more sisters than friends," she affirms and relates to a reading Sharon did for her years ago, when she predicted, "I could look forward to winning a lottery but that was long before the state of Georgia even had a lottery. I haven't yet won yet," she laughs, "but I will one day because I believe in Sharon."

It is because of friendship Jerrye opines that she can be completely honest and open about Sharon's gifts. Although her partner did not believe in psychics over the years, after the Lukander case in Florida, his attitude changed completely and later, when the Hardwick missing child case in Georgia became known, all doubt was erased. Jerrye explains she and her husband were driving to south Florida on their annual vacation when little Hayley Hardwick was reported missing by her father. They had no previous knowledge of the case.

"That night," she remembers, "I called Sharon to laughingly tell her I had missed winning the Saturday night lottery drawing, when she instantly related details regarding the missing baby. I wrote down everything she said just as she described what had happened to this little child, even to where she was buried. It was horrible to hear and it was incredulous when it took the Gwinnett County Police six weeks until they revealed the details Sharon had fully disclosed the actual day the baby went missing."

Jerrye recalls Sharon had a friend with the Gwinnett County Police force, who also tried to pass along Sharon's information; however, because it was revealed by a psychic, the officials were disinterested. "However, my partner who carefully followed this case and reviewed the notes I had written, certainly became a believer in Sharon's psychic power."

She again emphasizes how caring and giving Sharon is and describes her as a person who will help others even if it means she does without. "She loves with the biggest heart in the world and yet, she is physically, a tiny person. She cares for animals as she does for people, and is a Reiki master from whom I took a course. "She is an excellent teacher although I didn't give much thought to those lessons until nearly 15 years later, when a dear friend of mine was seriously injured in an automobile accident. She suffered severe emotional trauma which was seriously compounded when she was also told her father had only weeks to live. Her sleep was seriously impaired, so I had her sit in a recliner, covered her with a warm blanket and proceeded to perform the Reiki procedures Sharon had taught me. Within minutes, my friend fell fast asleep and once awakened, declared Reiki had helped her cope beyond the medical attention she had received. The lessons in Reiki Sharon had so patiently taught had once again proved profoundly beneficial."

Jerrye concludes, "It is impossible to describe how grateful I am to call Sharon my sister in this journey called life, but let me say I am blessed beyond description."

A FINAL NOTE

Sharon Johns lives nearby the town of Braselton, Georgia, which is 40 miles northeast of Atlanta, but when she speaks of rolling hills, verdant open fields, an abundance of mature trees, a gentle breeze that drifts in to cool the night and the sight of her horses running free on the soft green grass, you are aware the bucolic life is heaven on Earth for this psychic.

Her family, friends and her work fill her days and many evenings but she wouldn't have it any other way. Life is good for Sharon and she is good to everyone with whom she comes in contact. As she explained, her 'gift' comes from God and it is only by and through His blessings, that she can fulfill what she considers is the principal part of her purpose on earth.

Sharon is respected by her peers and loved by her clients, for whom she cares deeply. She has reached a place in her life when external cares and concerns tend to flitter away, as she makes every day worthwhile, whether it is at work or at play. She has been interviewed by Fox TV News, NBC News, Court TV, and is a popular subject for the print media, the why of which is obvious. In her soon to be published book, 'The Honey and the Sting' written with her friend and colleague, Mardeene Burr Mitchell, it is stated, "Sharon is fully capable of channeling, seeing past lives, talking to the deceased, talking with animals, talking with plants, talking with ghosts, seeing inside bodies and seeing into lives, as she intuits people's fears, feelings, hopes and dreams, to then advise whether it is in romance, business, career or relationship issues."

Sharon believes we must be in harmony with nature and ourselves too, because if we do life works out, but then again, only in God's good time. She chuckled when she added, "Well, it is true we do need to give Universe a nudge from time to time." Not to embellish nor diminish her story, let me add it is obvious Sharon lives in accordance with harmony, with herself, but most important of all, she lives according to God's own plan for her, which she terms the indisputable source of her serenity and her 'gift.'

For those who have read Sharon's story and might like to make contact:

Telephone: 770.965.9642

Email: happiness3@bellsouth.net

$85.00 for 30 minutes

rates are negotiable

CHARLATANS AND FRAUDS

BE CAREFUL... there is a downside to the psychic paradigm. Fraud exists and it is serious, so if you consider any communication with a psychic because as there is in every segment of society, the paranormal domain has its share of dishonorable and dishonest practitioners. You may know of several who are in the public eye by way of television, community venues and psychic functions where there may be those who will unfortunately prey on the lonely, the helpless, the bereaved and other people, desperately in need of direction and guidance.

There are numerous examples of psychics who are out for personal gain and who will to obtain it, promote readings, which tend to be more financially beneficial to them, rather than to provide assistance to their clients. For example, as reported by Steven Dubois of the Associated Press in February 2015, a psychic concocted an elaborate con to bilk millions of dollars from the heir to an Oregon timber fortune.

This woman, who will remain unnamed, used her teenage daughter, a blond wig, a fake accent, and a boy never born, to negotiate the theft of millions of dollars with the money directly deposited to her bank accounts. Her punishment, when the court case concluded, was eight years in a federal prison. In another case in Florida, a 62-year-old psychic scammed customers for almost $18 million, $12 million of which for 20 years, came from one client, who so desperately wanted contact with her deceased young son, did blindly accept as fact, that this fake psychic could arrange a connection for her through 'soul swapping.' Her punishment was ten years in federal prison.

In Texas, a woman was sentenced to two and half years on federal charges for wire fraud and money laundering after she operated a scam involving a psychic telephone line. Not only did she receive fees of several hundred dollars for her psychic counselling, but she also convinced her clients to send her money and property to be cleansed of evil.

A final example involved a Tarzana, California psychic and her husband, who faced criminal charges for allegedly bilking an emotionally vulnerable San Fernando Valley man of over $1 million, during the course of a two-year long scam.

There are other cases which detail unconditional fraud but the purpose of this warning is not to indict, but rather to support honourable psychics, whose sole purpose is to serve. It may also encourage potential clients to conduct their own diligent research before any decision is made to select a paranormal. Psychics, who practice ethical and accountable readings, will work arduously to ensure their primary purpose is to provide genuine guidance, comfort, counsel, or simply listen to clients, who trust and believe in them. References, tendered by clients can be easily researched and will confirm the accuracy and sincerity of a psychic.

These referrals are a sincere vindication of the individual ability of a specific reader. Each psychic featured in this narrative has tendered the same advice to those who are 'seekers'.

"Do your homework, be cautious and be sure to feel absolutely comfortable, before you make a final selection. The charlatans are out there, but they are in the minority."

Unfortunately, respectable practitioners must continue to repudiate the dishonorable people who are found in the psychic domain, but most assuredly, because they are aware of this, they, as the 'good guys,' diligently strive to protect their 'gifted' realm, by being ethical, honest and honourable.

Sources:

Association Press
Steven Dubois
February 2015
newser.com
Matt Cantor
March 4, 2014
wikipedia.org/wiki
Huffington Post

EARLY PSYCHICS . . .

Paranormal psychic phenomena are not new. They are centuries old and have been a source of study, investigation and controversy almost since the beginning of time. The Christian Bible and other early religions reference ghosts, demons and apparitions, all of which prominently influenced people, and were frequently the cause of superstition and bizarre behaviour.

For example, Sean Foster in his essay, 'The interesting History of Paranormal Investigation' states one of the earliest references to ghosts is found in the Old Testament, as it references the life of the prophet Samuel. Further, he says, Jesus Christ is even today referred to as 'Holy Ghost' but the early Greeks, Egyptians, Buddhist monks, and the ancient priests in India, also subscribed to paranormal practices.

In India and Tibet, the ancient religions of Hinduism, Buddhism and Jainism all subscribed to belief in reincarnation and karma. Reincarnation is explained as the belief that the soul, upon death of the body, comes back to earth in another body or form. Karma is the belief that all of your actions will have equal repercussions affecting you. It purports the theory is simply the universe runs according to certain laws, in other words, cause and effect. As paranormal phenomena continued its journey throughout the years, numerous psychics became popular throughout history, including but not limited to, Nostradamus (1503-1566), Amicus Bartholomeus (1562-1649), Arthur Stormberger Eighteenth Century, Edgar Cayce (1877-1945), who was born in Beverly, Kentucky, and called a mystic and a clairvoyant. He is considered by many to be the father of holistic medicine, and is named the most documented psychic of the 20th century, although his psychic abilities were often questioned by skeptics.

Sources:

Kevin Williams - near-death.com
urban dictionary.com
dictionary.reference.com
ghoststory.com
wikipedia.org/wiki/Bartholomeus_Amicus
Doug Webber - A Prophecy of World War 111 (Stormberger)
wikipedia.org/wikiEdgar_Cayce

GLOSSARY

In this book about psychics, there are words and expressions which may be unfamiliar or strange, especially if The Reader is new to the world of the paranormal. The following list will define some but not all of the phrases and names used by psychics, mediums and their colleagues. Although they may not be found in this book, they are commonplace in the world of psychic/mediums. Meanings vary, but in the cause of expediency, meanings will define the more familiar usage, although in some instances to ensure understanding, a more complete explanation is proffered.

Psychic - clairvoyant, mystic, sensitive

Medium - a seer, a vehicle, a clairvoyant

Ghostlike - unnatural or unearthly

Portal - a doorway or entry into the paranormal

Transchanneling - a method of transforming a portion of energy from a higher level being

Deep trance channeling - a deep trance state wherein a person who is able to set their conscious self aside in order to allow a spirit to speak through their body

Occult - esoteric, mystic, preternatural. Sometimes referred to as parasites who can infiltrate this earth to feed off human energy. It is said the United States has deep occult roots. These parasites can be exceedingly noisy, loud and are capable of psychically attacking a human being. Changes in behavior, severe headaches upon awakening in the morning and extreme agitation can be their calling card

Spiritualism - communication between the living and the dead

Poltergeist - makes strange sounds and movements

Possession - one who is in the grip of something demonic

Reiki - derived from Japanese words - Rei - which means God's Wisdom or the Higher Power, and Ki - life force energy . . . therefore Reiki means spiritually, guided life force energy

Séance - an attempt to communicate with Spirits. derived from the French word for 'seat or 'session' or 'sitting.' In English this word is usual specifically for a meeting of people who are gathered to receive messages from Spirits, whose energy is invited in provide closure or to healing to the living

Kinetic energy - description for the movement of objects by a ghost or poltergeists (German for noisy ghost) who can move, throw or destroy property

Anomaly - an image found on a picture, photograph, video or voice recording that has no explainable source

Apparition - a spirit that manifest in human form and is visible to the human eye, often in period clothing

Ectoplasm - smoke or fog-like mist sometimes seen in photos or large groups of people but difficult to define

Orb - believed to be the energy or the spirit and soul of enlightened individuals, who manifest as circles or balls of light in photos. The brighter the light denotes their knowledge of truth

Shadow people or Dark Shadows - detectable by the naked eye, believed by some to be demons but by others as departed souls who have yet to pass into the light. Because they have they do not recognize truth but cling to falsity, and they can be combative when spotted

Tarot - any of a set of 78 cards, 22 playing cards called Major Arcana and 56 suit cards known as the Minor Arcana. Bearing allegorical representations, used for fortune telling. Also a card in a tarot pack with distinctive symbolic design, such as the Wheel of Fortune. Tarot began in Europe as a card game, but used to gain insight into a person's life. Jeanne Mayell, tarot reader and a psychotherapist in Boston area predicts Hillary Clinton will win the presidency, and will wear a blue suit and blue hat on inauguration day

Aurora - a natural light display in the sky caused by particles in the atmosphere, i.e. Northern Lights, however, the meaning and spelling takes on a dissimilar explanation when used in the paranormal domain

The Aura: The Paranormal - in parapsychology and spiritual practice, an aura is a field of subtle, luminous radiation surrounding a person or object like the halo or aureola in religious art. It is said all living things manifest an aura which is the subtle energy field to which people who meet for the first time will credit or discredit an aura as to their instant like or dislike of someone. There is no scientific definition for an aura as many scientists are certain they do not exist. The human aura is also sometimes referred to as a psychic energy field

Supernatural - unreal such as ghost images, haunted homes, EVP investigations, even the Ouija Board

Spirit - a spirit is an entity who never had a body

Ghost - dates back to ancestor worship in pre-literate times, and sometimes known as a specter. Considered the soul or spirit of a dead person or animal that can appear in visible form or other manifestation of the living and capable of haunting particular locations objects and people

Light Worker - any being dedicated to the cultivation of inner presence and elevation of awareness in self and others. Also known as oriental Chi, Yin and Yang

Palmistry - known as hand analysis which is the most powerful and complete system of self-knowledge. Everything about you is revealed in your hands. It is a precise science that reveals the career for which you are suited. It also gives a complete understanding of your emotional, creative and spiritual direction. Hand analysis is by far the most scientific and dependable system of self-awareness

Psychic Energy - an actuating force or factor or described as mental energy or the psychological feature that arouses an organism to action toward a desire goal or the reason for the action

Spirit Guide - an entity which provides spiritual guidance through channeling or a medium...which can manifest by a very strong feeling, a picture in our minds or even a voice in our heads

Materializations - the rarest of all reported paranormal physical phenomena which manifest as hands that move, bodies that speak

Angel - The word angel means messenger but their communication is one-way. They do not want to be relied upon or revered by human beings

Demonic entity - Sometimes referred to as the devil, Satan, Lucifer, who omit a putrid odour as they slink around through walls onto floors. They often appear as 'black smoke' and are frightening to all who witness them

Ectoplasm - during a séance, ectoplasm can stream from a medium's mouth, pool on the floor and then becomes a body part or whole person, and further explained as it is said to be repulsive and often appears to be milky white in colour and smell like ozone

Fortune telling fraud - a method used by a fortune teller who uses cold reading skills to detect clients who are genuinely troubled but told they are cursed, but for a fee the curse can be removed

Soul Attachment - a soul may attach itself to a vulnerable person because the soul may have unfulfilled wishes. Lack of clarity of mind can be an invitation for a soul to enter a body, but can be expelled if they are told in a loud voice to leave. More than one soul can occupy the same body

Top Hat Man - considered a demonic presence who can look similar to a shadow person, but may appear in solid form. He can look quite dapper as he sports a gaucho, top or cowboy hat, and often wears a three-piece suit with a chain watch seen in the pocket. However, his glowing red eyes and a pointed chin and nose will ensure he is exactly as noted, Top Hat Man, whose purpose is to instill fear or actually cause physical pain

Sensitive - one who is responsive to another's feelings, fears, trials and tribulations. Although there are fewer of them, there is a category here called voice natural direct sensitive who can hear people's voices and see inside their lives and past history

Soul swapping - can occur when one soul departs a body to be replaced by another, perhaps after an accident, or when a person is unconscious and will happen so quietly that the person will not know it occurred. If a person is extremely angry or in constant personal conflict they can be vulnerable to soul swapping.

Source:
SimonaRich.com/soul-attachment

NOTE:

Words and definitions
in the glossary found in:
Wikipedia
Oahu Ghost Tours
Psychic Networks
Individual psychics
dictionary.reference.com
General research sites
Sikh Philosophy Network
Mike Sententia - www.magicofthought.com
lightworkers.org
Jeanne Mayell - tarot reader/psychotherapist
aprilcrawford.com
psychiclibrary.com
thefreedictionary.com
Professor JanVandersande - physicist
www.urbandictionary.com
simonarich.com

READING CHOICES

In the supernatural field of psychic interpretation, there are four, it not more choices, when it comes to the types of reading performed.

The following describes those options.

COLD READING:

This reading comprises general presumption that is applicable to every person. It is when a psychic will provide all of the messages received and you do not offer any information at all.

WARM READING:

Generalities are revealed which can apply to almost everyone and anyone, but if one believes in the paranormal, i.e., horoscopes – they are especially good candidates, and are more likely to believe in vague generalities. To explain further, it is relevant to a warm-up chat with you where a psychic can glean information from what you say, even though you may be unaware you said anything at all that was pertinent or of interest.

HOT READING:

Information garnered prior to a reading by a colleague of the psychic, who will surreptitiously impart what has been learned to the psychic but kept from the client. This is often referred to as the use of 'foreknowledge.'

HONEST READING:

Considered effective and factual because the psychic requests a client reveal only a first name, and proffer no additional personal information in the reading. A true psychic will never ask you questions before or during a reading. Psychics are referred to as sensitives, because as the name implies, they must be responsive to your feelings. If they are to 'tune into' Spirits, they must first connect with you.

ONE FINAL QUESTION...

If you have reached this place in the book, it will mean I hope that you have read it through, that you have been entertained and finally that you have formed your own opinions about the viability of psychics. Perhaps you will have decided you agree with a Calgary, Alberta radio announcer, who believes every aspect of the paranormal is 'simply hogwash' or you may have decided you want to visit one to determine exactly what occurs in this spectral world.

You may even go so far as to arrange a reading, or you may want to research this unfathomable domain for yourself. However, there can be no denying this is a burgeoning phenomenon today, as more and more people seek the services of a psychic. But then again, you may simply close the book to end this journey.

Before you go, there was one final question I put to each psychic and although I will not specifically identify the individual replies, you may find the predictions interesting. Before I reveal the question, here is an explanation as to why it was asked. My husband and I, after what has been a lifetime, have called home one of earth's most beautiful, quiet, pastoral places to be found anywhere.

We have travelled extensively from Hawaii to Australia, but sad to say, it is time to move on, downsize, and settle elsewhere. Such decisions are difficult but our time for change is here. Thinking some foreknowledge would be helpful, I therefore put this question to each psychic:

Can you foresee when our properties will sell by month and year?

Every one of the psychics offered a different time line, some of which have passed, others are yet to come, but it is interesting to note such revelations are obviously difficult to render. This script is being written early in summer, 2015, and to this date, the properties remain for sale. It isn't over and who knows but there will be a psychic whose prediction regarding a sale will be spot on.

Does this fact in any way affect my feelings about psychics? The answer is a complicated yes and no, because my opinion is not solely based on the one and only one personal question I asked. Admittedly, had the predictions worked out, the task of selling and moving would be over, but despite the inaccurate predictions, my confidence and belief in the psychics found in this book is steady. Despite the many hours of interviews, despite the sincerity of the psychics herein, despite all I have read and researched and despite all the testimonials gathered from numerous others, I am still skeptical. I remain confused and still question the fundamentals of this dimension known as the supernatural. But I keep an open mind and will, as this narrative is almost finished. I will, for the first time, consider initiating a reading of my own. I did not do this prior to, or during the writing of this story, to ensure my mind was kept clear of possible psychic suggestions and influences if they exist, but further, I wanted to limit my own prejudices about the supernatural. I also did not access the websites of any psychic featured herein or any other for that matter.

I hope I have accomplished my objective.

EPILOGUE...

The research is done, the interviews are over, the book is written and as this two-year-plus project draws down, here are final thoughts about the psychic phenomenon garnered over countless interviews and an endless search for fact, separated from fiction, in this esoteric domain.

It is difficult to explain why immeasurable people from every walk of life believe in and subscribe to the guidance and assistance they find in the psychic sphere. It can be said, nonetheless, there are thousands and thousands of people everywhere who do believe, who are committed and live their lives according to the frequent suggestions and admonitions received in readings from their chosen psychics.

The one lesson learned is the fact there is no shortage of people who believe unequivocally in the paranormal and find the advance warnings or advice they receive, to be exceedingly helpful in their day-to-day lives. If you are curious as why this is, perhaps a partial explanation is this. As people move away from the more traditional religious practices there may be a void, which is aptly filled by their own personal psychic. To this writer, it is absolutely indisputable to state the paranormal paradigm has origins which began centuries ago, but is as relevant and prevalent today as psychics continue to garner popularity which stretches from small towns to big cities the world over. Psychics are found everywhere. In their attempt to attract clients, there are those who frequently claim to be to be more capable and competent than the one previous. They can be found at various functions from fairs, expositions and special events, all of which are hugely popular and well attended.

For example, the weekend of March 20, 2015, if you had been in Phoenix, Arizona, you could have attended a Psychic Fair that offered psychic readings, Tarot, Palmistry, Past Lives, Spirit Mediums and Clairvoyants. However, if you had wanted a reading at this event, the developer noted early arrangements would have been necessary, because they were solidly booked days in advance. A reading at this event cost $45 for a half hour and this amount increased by five dollars if paid by credit card, or it cost $70 for one hour, but you had your choice of five psychics for the session. If Phoenix wasn't in your travel plans back then, there would have been no reason to lament missing it, because there were also fairs in Red Deer, Alberta, Belleville, Ontario, Regina, Sask., Medicine Hat, Alberta, Hamilton, Ontario, and numerous cities in California, Florida, Nevada, Utah, Kentucky, New Jersey, and other cities across the United States and Canada, and each one was scheduled for March 2015.

Take heart if you missed one because those same psychic fairs will be repeated every year for years to come, as long as the people attend. Endless psychic festivals are scheduled across North America throughout this year, because psychics and psychic fairs are ubiquitous. The trick, however, is to find the right paranormal in the right venue, where you will be comfortable, secure, and confident you are in safe hands, as you have your mind read and your future predicted. In her enthralling book, 'The Wheel of Fortune' British author, Susan Howatch observes through her character, Dr. Pamela Mallinson, quote, "I believe there are different ways of looking at a given situation and none of these ways need necessarily be invalid. But I do think the classification 'paranormal' should be reserved for those situations which can't be explained rationally."

In her philosophy, I couldn't agree more. It is impossible to explain in a more succinct way the unusual and uncanny information I have researched and/or have gleaned from the five psychics in this book. There are mystical experiences which cannot be explained but paradoxically, there may be other revelations which might be considered simple deductions. But how to explain psychic phenomena as it is used in crime resolution, especially murder, is difficult and one cannot refute the eerie paranormal potency.

I have been asked by those who are aware this book is upcoming, if I have had a psychic reading. No, as explained earlier, I have not, although each psychic interviewed did ask to 'read' me, but it was important to approach this subject as an uninformed novice. Ergo; as stated, I rejected anything overly influential during my investigation of these paranormal phenomena. The question, "Will I now get a reading?" I now reply, "I don't know. Perhaps! Maybe!" But if I do it will be kept private and confidential. In the years it has taken to research and write this book, one fact is certain, which is to follow my own warning to be cautious in my selection of a psychic. I would readily choose any one of those featured in this narrative, because each one of them has passed the charlatan/fraud test. They are real. They care about their clients and they believe their 'gift' comes from a higher power.

You, Dear Reader, will determine whether you believe in the paranormal and can accept predictions from a psychic, but as for me despite some reservations, there is so much I have learned which is inexplicable in this profession. Based on fact, it is difficult for me to discredit at least portions of this uncanny sphere, or demean those people, who can predict the future or define the past. As stated, your perspective is your decision.

The End

ACKNOWLEDGEMENTS

Writing Seeing Things… was a challenge mostly because life is frenetic, but this book would not have materialized without the inspiration of Lisa, and the cooperation of each psychic, who freely shared private, personal and professional details about their lives with me.

I owe a debt of gratitude to them, to Gary and to Len, for their patient and expert technical assistance, special thanks to David, for what is a writer without the attention and care of a demanding editor. You have my profound appreciation and finally to friends, whose interest has never wavered nor did their enquiry as to how I was doing and when the book would be published. Here it is.

I hope you enjoy.

CPSIA information can be obtained
at www.ICGtesting.com
Printed in the USA
FSOW02n0810230116
15860FS